FREELA

HOW TO MAKE
MONEY

PETER SAXTON SCHROEDER

Published by Richter Publishing LLC
www.richterpublishing.com

Book Cover Design: Jessie Alarcon

Editor: Margarita Martinez

Book Formatting: Monica San Nicolas

ISBN-13: 978-1-954094-17-8 Paperback

DISCLAIMER

ACKNOWLEDGMENTS

I wish to express my gratitude to

my writing colleagues at

OWAA (Outdoor Writers Association of America),

NOWA (Northwest Outdoor Writers Association),

OWAC (Outdoor Writers Association of California),

and other writers organizations, who attended my

lectures over the years and

encouraged me to compile them into this book.

CONTENTS

DEDICATION

This book is dedicated to all freelance writers who
have the grit to pursue their dreams of writing about
what is meaningful to them.
They work without a net.
Alone.
On their own they pitch ideas to harried editors,
spend hours researching and writing articles,
deal with corporate lawyers, and negotiate with
publishers to get paid on time.
After all this hassle, you deserve financial success.

INTRODUCTION

The best thing I did when I set out to become a freelance outdoors travel writer: not quitting my day job.

My biggest mistake: buying all the books about how to be a full-time writer. When following the recommendations of these authors, all I did was waste money and become frustrated. It took three years to understand how wrong all those recommendations were.

It's not that I was unsuccessful. I got many writing assignments during those first three years, but they lacked focus. At best, each writing job was breakeven. At worst, and that was most of those projects, it cost me more to complete each assignment than I earned. I'm glad I held onto my day job so I could pay for this high-priced learning experience.

Many things I tried didn't work, but along the way I began to figure out what did work. That's when I eventually made a profitable business out of what was previously an expensive hobby.

Soon I was making a more-than-comfortable income. Over the years my approach made it possible to visit—for free—more than 100 countries, including every major ski resort, numerous sailing-cruise venues, and countless adventure-travel destinations across the globe.

This book is a distillation of what I learned, and—spoiler alert—it contradicts much of what traditional books tell you to do. Here's my take on how you, too, can make money as a freelance writer.

1
THE EMPOWERED WRITER

From my perspective, the main value of being a freelance writer is the lifestyle—one that keeps the "free" in freelancer.

Ideal Lifestyle

Do you desire a lifestyle that allows you to do what you want to do when you want to do it, with no restrictions except of your own making? Even a Fortune 500 CEO doesn't have the freedom of a freelancer who is responsible only for and to oneself.

Just imagine the advantages:

- No messy personnel problems requiring attention.

- No policy and procedure manuals dictating behavior.

- No background office chatter or interruptions by well-meaning colleagues.

- No mandated dress codes. (Who's going to object if you work in your bathrobe all morning or take a midafternoon nap?)

- No schedules to be followed or meetings to attend.

- And none of the money you earn will be snatched away prematurely in payroll deductions for taxes, social security, insurance premiums, and other items. You can keep that money and use it for yourself until payments are due.

You can take coffee breaks, eat lunch, or close up shop anytime you want. You can schedule haircuts, shopping trips, and doctor appointments whenever you wish. Who cares whether you shaved or put on makeup (except if you have a Zoom call)? And you can attune your work hours to your personal rhythms, which in my case often change. Sometimes I rise early to start the workday at 5 a.m. Other times I'll be on my computer late at night until 2 or 3 a.m. If the sun is shining on a Wednesday, I might go sailing or hiking in the mountains. On a rainy weekend I'll often work through both days. Best of all, I don't have to decide ahead of time what I'm going to do. Short of self-imposed restrictions, I am free to lead a spontaneous life.

No Commute

But the lifestyle is only one of many advantages of being a freelance writer. What about the daily commute? With an office in my home, it takes less than a minute to go to and from work. Tell that to friends who are often stuck in hours-long traffic twice each day! And it's not just the savings in wasted time. Think about the environment, cost of gas, and wear and tear on the car. Furthermore, no commute means no risk of a traffic accident.

Home Advantages

Working from home has other benefits. You're among familiar surroundings of your own choosing rather than in an impersonal room full of office furnishings. Because your career is part of your lifestyle, you can bounce from one to the other in minutes. My workstation can alternate from my office to the living room and out to the back patio over the course of a day. Want a cup of coffee, a midmorning snack, or a sandwich? Just trundle into your kitchen and make it. What could be handier?

Tax Benefits

Working from a home office is not only convenient; it also offers tax advantages. Unlike when you work in a company office, every expense related to your home office is tax deductible, including the portion of your mortgage and home insurance allocable to your work space. Expenses such as office supplies, telecommunications, maintenance, office equipment, utilities, and work-related travel are all allowable tax deductions.

As a general rule, the IRS likes to see a profit in three of every five years. However, this isn't a hard and fast rule. Rather, it's important to show the intent to make a profit, which may take longer. Furthermore, some years will be good and some will be bad, so fluctuation of profit and loss is not uncommon. For example, if a major health problem curtails the time you can work, or if you lose some markets and need time to recoup, the IRS is not so restrictive. It's also understandable if you incur expenses on an assignment that puts you into the red for the year, because payment isn't forthcoming until the following year.

Personal Expression

Apart from these tangible benefits of freelance writing, there are psychological benefits that many consider most important of all. Freelance writing lets you express to the world who you are and what you believe in, all while supporting the causes and passions that inspire you. Somewhere a media outlet exists for any subject you can imagine. If you're into saving, protecting, safeguarding, or defending something, you can find publications that welcome articles about whales, wolves, redwoods, clean water, elephants, and the wilderness. If you feel passionate about issues such as gay rights, women's equality, population control, recycling, climate change, or gun control, you can find publications that welcome articles on these topics. Want to ban something? How about pesticides, nuclear testing, nonbiodegradable plastics, abortion, or automatic weapons?

In addition, consider all the markets for articles about recreation. Are you into biking, skiing, running, rock climbing, fishing, hunting, hang gliding, gardening, scuba diving, sailing, surfing, or camping? Hobby magazines seek pieces about pottery, weaving, woodworking, stamp collecting, jewelry making, and auto repair. Somewhere in this litany of ideas is your opportunity to go deeper into your personal interests.

As for me, I write about my own passions: downhill skiing, destination bareboat cruising under sail, scuba diving, and adventure travel. By leveraging these interests, I have been able to pursue them all over the globe. Later in my career I expanded beyond my usual interests into areas I wanted to know about. That's how I learned about and wrote articles covering biking and barging the rivers of Europe, winemaking, wildlife viewing, and photography.

Business Building

There is, nevertheless, a downside to these benefits. When I started freelance writing more than 30 years ago, I felt prepared to deal with the demands of this work: I could handle tight deadlines, long hours at my keyboard, and the vicissitudes of editors. I was, however, unwilling to accept the extremely low pay that seemed to be inherent in this work. In any other career, the same level of effort would command double or triple the income. Yet when mentioning this unfair pay scale to other writers, I was often met with a shrug of the shoulders.

Freelancers often feel there's a certain nobility in the acceptance of poverty as the price to pay for doing work they love. Initially I, too, adopted this acceptance of sacrifice and hardship. I'd complain and whine, but my grumbling wasn't genuine. Rather it was an ironic acknowledgment that this work combined a meaningful career with a wonderful lifestyle.

But in time I found this poverty mentality to be a myth. There's plenty of money to be made if you approach the creativity of freelancing with the bottom-line realism of accounting. It boils down to empowering yourself and adhering to a simple truism—maximize income/minimize costs.

How-(Not)-To Books

All the other how-to books I read (and I read a lot of them!) fall short, because they address only the writing side of the equation but ignore the money-making side.

They fail to show how to turn freelance writing into a business. This is what I will explain in the following chapters.

2
GETTING STARTED

All I knew when I started was a little bit about grammar. I didn't know how magazines and newspapers (websites didn't exist yet) operated, and I knew nothing about how to work with editors. I wasn't familiar with deadlines, contracts, queries, pay scales, or legal aspects of the writing business. But I was determined to become a writer and thought I was smart enough to figure all this out along the way. And yes, figure it out I did, but I learned the hard way.

Why I Became a Writer

But why, exactly, did I want to be a writer? After having invested eight years in earning bachelor and master of science degrees and a master of business administration, I was in the midst of a successful career in engineering management. So why leave a successful career in a field for which I was well-trained and experienced?

First, I was dissatisfied with my present career; second, I had derived great satisfaction years earlier from writing an article for a major metropolitan newspaper about a summer adventure. Let me digress a moment and reflect upon this pivotal article.

Seeking a summer adventure after graduating from an East Coast university, a classmate and I hired ourselves out to a contract service to deliver cars from New York to Seattle, which would one day be my home when I had a family. When we went our separate ways after spending a few weeks at our destination, I hitchhiked down the coast to San Francisco to visit friends before setting out to thumb rides back east to my family in Louisville, Kentucky. On one of my rides departing the Bay Area, my benefactor suggested it would be more interesting if I hopped freight trains across the country. I asked him to tell me more. After explaining the rudiments of the process, he dropped me off near the Union Pacific freight terminal in Sacramento, which is where my article begins.

The following three weeks I had the adventure of a lifetime jumping on and off trains as they threaded across deserts and mountain ranges through more than a dozen states before reaching Louisville. Along the way I met colorful characters like the one who said I was a damn fool for turning my back on him because he could have pushed me off a flatbed car traveling 60 miles per hour so he could steal my meager belongings. Another time I was almost scorched to death riding atop a box car. When the train entered a tunnel, the burning cinders and hot gases from the engines set my lungs afire. If I hadn't had the sense to dive into my sleeping bag, I'm not sure I would be here today. From then on, I learned to jump on a car far back from the engines.

Through such adventures I learned the lore and lure of riding the rails. Once home, I was so overwhelmed with these experiences that I had to write them down. I pounded them (remember the old typewriters?) into an article that found its way to an editor's desk at my hometown newspaper.

The editor liked the story and assigned a newspaper photographer to take photos of me in the local freight yards, simulating different maneuvers acquired during my travels. When the article appeared in print, I felt elated and proud—feelings I never experienced in my engineering career. Something told me back then that one day I would be a writer.

In retrospect, I realize I had stumbled across a two-step rhythm that would be the key to my future as a freelance writer. First step is to venture out "there" to explore. Second, return to the quiet of "home" to reflect and weave the details of the experience into a story. It's a rhythm of going into the hectic universe for a unique experience, then returning to a quiet, meditative state to reflect, recall, and record not just the events, but also the feelings and near-hidden meanings of whatever else was going on. From "marketplace to meditation."

Letters to the Editor

Now, back to figuring out how to become a writer. I was motivated but didn't have the tools. How should I start?

In order to try to get my name in front of the people hiring writers, I decided to write letters to the editor. Knowing I would need to find a controversial subject to garner the desired attention, I lit upon an idea when I stumbled across an article in the travel section of my hometown Seattle newspaper about the indigenous peoples of the Northwest. The article made reference to totem poles of the U.S. and Canadian tribes. However, totem poles are found only in Canada, not within the societies of the native peoples in the U.S.

Wanting to be clever, I headed my letter "Totemic Trouble" and explained the error with reference to "Totemic Tourism." The *Seattle Times* newspaper ran my letter, and the letters editor called to thank me for catching this error. Seemed like an auspicious sign.

When another article incorrectly identified a wolf eel as an eel although it is, in fact, a fish, I sent a correction letter that the editor promptly published.

As a lifelong sailor familiar with sailboat designs in the Pacific Northwest, I found an error in another article that incorrectly identified a keel as a center board. Off went a letter to the same editor, and a few days later it was published. Each time I telephoned and thanked her for running my corrections, and soon we became phone buddies.

When a non-sailing reporter for the newspaper covered a local regatta, I telephoned and explained the shortcomings in his article. With nine sailing Olympians and hundreds of sailing enthusiasts living in Seattle, they all must have had a good laugh when they read the article. Shortly afterward, the editor, embarrassed by this mix-up, called back to ask if I would write a short news piece on the upcoming Whidbey Island Race Week, the premier sailing regatta in the Pacific Northwest. Suddenly I had my first real assignment: 500 words for $125.

I wrote similar letters to the editor of the Canadian boating magazine *Pacific Yachting*. Not much response for several months until one missive I sent stirred up quite a storm. When an article appeared about a group of Vancouver sailors who cruised in the northern Vava'u archipelago of Tonga, I was interested because I had bareboat chartered there several years earlier. The charterers, thinking they were spreading happiness among the children, described distributing candy and plastic toys in the villages.

Infuriated, I wrote a letter to the editor pointing out that these people lived a subsistence lifestyle with pigs and goats running freely throughout the village and had no dental or medical facilities. Introducing sweets and knickknacks from the developed world disrupted their lifestyle and created health hazards. Letters came flying back in the next issue, noting the charterers were just trying to be helpful, but this prompted another letter from me and from others who supported my position. The rankling continued for months.

Additional Assignments

The Canadian editor telephoned to thank me for stirring up this controversy, which publications love because it tends to increase sales. When our conversation got around to my interests in writing, he asked if I would submit a news article with a tight deadline about the recent sinking of a sailing yacht on the west coast of Vancouver Island in which two lives had been lost. Having no idea what this entailed, I nevertheless immediately accepted, thereby garnering my second paid assignment. And it wasn't long after that before he assigned me to write a feature article, the first of many to come.

The point is there are many ways to get started, but the letters-to-the-editor route worked for me. Once I had fulfilled a couple of assignments, I had the credentials—the "clips" and references—needed to approach other publications.

Let's say you've stumbled into a couple of assignments the way I did. Now is the time to decide if you want to go forward as a freelancer or if, dissuaded by the hassles, you're ready to abandon the effort.

Home Office

If you're still committed, it's time to get your basic setup in order. Considering you'll be spending hours at a time in a creative mindset, you'll need a well-equipped, dedicated office that is away from distractions and noise. Once assignments begin to arrive, you don't want to be caught without the basic tools: desk, filing cabinet, bookshelf, office chair, and storage unit for office supplies. Chances are you'll be conducting telephone interviews, so check the laws in your state to learn how to record conversations legally. If you ever become entangled in a legal or libel matter, a record of your discussions could become valuable evidence. And once you make it into the big time, major news organizations like the *New York Times* or the *Atlantic* require backup notes and recordings from their journalists.

As I explain in a later chapter, taking your own photos to illustrate your articles increases your income—hugely. You should buy basic photographic equipment. While it need not be top-level professional gear, it should have adequate resolution for images suitable for printing in high-quality publications. Of the top two camera brands, Nikon and Canon, I started out with Nikon and continue with its equipment today. Because I shoot a lot of images aboard boats in a salt-spray environment, I originally chose Nikon because its cameras were said to be more waterproof because the electronics were better protected than Canon's. That difference isn't true today (and maybe never was), but as I added more filters, lenses, and other accessories over time, I was loath to change brands—particularly after Nikon made me a member of its Nikon Professional Services, entitling me to discounts, special offers, free loaner equipment, and training services.

Next, you need a computer, of course, a current version of Adobe Acrobat Reader, and supporting software for writers. I'm a PC guy with the latest version of Windows and Office 365, which offers everything I need.

Now it's time to reach out to potential markets.

3
FINDING MARKETS

Although many beginning writers struggle to identify markets for their work, locating them is straightforward. Bear in mind, however, that finding potential outlets and getting your stories published are quite different. Pitching an article is (relatively) easy. Getting an editor to accept your query is far more difficult.

Market Sources

All Freelance Writing (allfreelancewriting.com) is arguably the leading resource to find publications that will accept articles from freelancers. AFW lists several hundred magazines that pay for freelance work, and access to these listings is free. To narrow your research, publications are broken into categories: sports, recreation, lifestyle, religion, hobbies, and more. Each listing gives a short profile of every publication along with pay rates, writer guidelines, types of articles needed, how to query, editor contact, and other information. You can also post your profile and writing specialty in hopes that an editor will reach out to you. The AFW website includes helpful tutorials, advice, tips, and how-to articles for writers of every level. You can also submit questions and get writing advice.

A Google search will turn up numerous additional opportunities for freelance writing outlets. Various sources for freelance writing work, such as freelance writing job sites, will connect writers with organizations that need writers either for specific assignments or for long-term work.

For newspapers, a search on the internet of the 100 largest newspapers in North America, or leading newspapers of any country, will turn up circulation figures, editor contacts, writer guidelines, and editorial calendars.

Professional writers groups, such as Society of American Travel Writers (SATW), Outdoor Writers Association of America (OWAA), Boating Writers International (BWI), North American Snowsports Journalists Association (NASJA), Ski Club of International Journalists (SCIJ), and others list market opportunities in their newsletters.

One of the best sources for finding writing markets is your neighborhood bookstore or newsstand. I regularly purchase magazines related to my specialties to keep track of new publications on the market as well as to remain current with changes of editor positions. Not only do I learn editor contacts from the mastheads, but I also become familiar with the types of articles they run. Even more important, I glean ideas from their advertisers for articles I could write that support their products.

Many publications publish editorial calendars that focus on particular themes for specific editions. If a magazine dedicates its September issue to Hawaii or its March edition to bicycling, the editors will be seeking related articles up to a year in advance.

Knowing how and when to break in is critical to getting an assignment, so don't try to pitch a story in July expecting it to be accepted for the September issue. Although there is much variation, magazines typically assign articles six to eight months in advance of the publication date. Newspapers have greater latitude and can assign articles six months to six minutes in advance.

Read several issues of a publication and know who the advertisers are before contacting the editor. Don't expect to sell a gun-control piece to a publication that carries advertisements for ammunition. And steer clear of submissions about teenage culture if a publication runs ads for hearing aids and reading glasses. Don't submit an article written in third person when all the stories in a magazine are first person, and if the average length of an article is 500 words, don't try to pitch a 1,500-word piece.

Editor Contacts

By now you know the publications you want to approach and the subject you want to propose. You know the demographics of their readership, the products of the advertisers, and the typical length and writing style of the articles they publish. Next, it's time to develop and send your query.

When I started years ago, I sent—by U.S. postal mail—one query to one publication and waited for a reply, just as the how-to writing books said I should. Nothing came back, so after four weeks I followed up with another request and this time received a terse reply that the publication wasn't interested. Next, I queried another magazine and repeated the cycle that resulted in yet another rejection. A third try, a third rejection. But this is how the experts said I should do it.

I subsequently learned what was really happening. My query initially landed on the desk of an intern or a junior editor. If he or she liked it, it was forwarded to the next level up. If not, it was put aside to one day send a rejection notice. Same procedure with the next higher editors until my query reached the top level, where it remained until someone made a final decision. If my query arrived when everyone was on deadline, it would languish until someone got it moving through the system. So much for the great advice I had read.

Forget what the so-called experts tell you. Here's an approach that works for me and gets a quick turnaround. First step is to telephone the publication—which the other how-to books say never to do—and ask for the name and telephone number of the editor who handles freelance submissions. I then call this person directly. If I get voice mail, I hang up. Never leave a message. You, as an unknown, will never get a return call. I try again later and, if necessary, repeat this periodically in the days ahead.

If or when the editor picks up the phone, I briefly introduce myself as a sailing journalist and ask an innocent question:

"Are you the editor who handles freelance submissions?" which I already know is true.

Receiving an affirmative answer, I quickly say something like, "Thanks, I'll be sending you a query for an article about a bareboat charter cruise in Tahiti that I recently completed."

You will get one of these three responses:

"No thanks. We recently covered Tahiti. We're not interested."

"Thanks, send it in; I'll look for it."

"Tahiti, hmmm; tell me about your cruise?"

To the first response, I express appreciation and we say goodbye without wasting each other's time. To the second, I say thanks and goodbye but will reference this conversation when I submit the query. To the third response, I'm in luck, because now I have a chance to elaborate about the cruise. The editor may then want to know more about, for example, the marae, the sacred stone temples, which I, of course, say will be included in my article. Even if I never previously heard of or saw them, I can research the information I need. We conclude the conversation with my saying that I will send a query. My query will have a better chance of receiving attention now that the editor and I have established a bond.

However brief, the phone call with an editor, who responds with either "maybe" or "tell me more," gives me the right to query this editor directly. I begin my email with the line: "Dear (name), I enjoyed our telephone conversation on (date) when we discussed my recent bareboat charter cruise in Tahiti." Because the email is personal, it bypasses the rungs of lower editors who might reject my query. Since the editor could have forgotten our short conversation, my first sentence reminds her about cruising in Tahiti. As mentioned, the how-to books advise not to try this direct approach; nonetheless, personal experience has shown it creates an opening for me to continue.

Queries

The query itself should consist of five (only five) short paragraphs. I whimsically call my approach, which is different from what the how-to books advise, "Quintessential Queries for the Querulous Editor."

Remember: freelance writing is not all about creativity. It's about marketing and making money. Therefore, the first paragraph of any query should do what every good marketing executive accomplishes with products from toothpaste to perfume: give a sample. In this case give an example of your writing to hook the editor. A good practice is to start with the lede (lead) to the article you are proposing.

Here's a lede I used for a fishing article: *When my guide met me on the dock, he asked, "Do you want to go fishing...or do you want to catch fish? There is a difference."* The reader will be curious enough to continue into the next sentence to understand what the guide means.

Or for the Tahiti query: *Two slab-sided peaks jut above the tropical sea's horizon. Blurred by trade-wind haze, the silhouettes push into billowy clouds tinged pale green from the reflection of the jungled slopes. No wonder sailors describe their approach toward shrine-like Bora Bora as a pilgrimage.*

Sometimes quotes are effective, such as this opener for an article about cross-country skiing in Yellowstone:

"Would you rather be among three million people who visit the Park in summer or just 100,000 who arrive in winter?" asked Rick Hoeninghausen, director of sales and marketing for Xanterra Parks & Resorts, which runs concessions in Yellowstone National Park. While guiding our group on cross-country skis through Yellowstone last winter, Hoenighausen continued, "With fewer people, it's quieter in winter. There are no cars, and animals are easier to spot against the snow with no leaves on the trees to block views. Herds come down from the mountains and you see more wildlife in the meadows: bobcats, antelope, foxes, and bison."

In a couple of sentences I've demonstrated my writing style and given high points of the proposed article.

The second paragraph in the query should describe the article. For the cruise in Tahiti it might begin: *I propose an article about a bareboat charter cruise on a 42-foot Beneteau in Tahiti, starting in Raiatea and encircling the leeward islands of Huahine, Taha'a, and Bora Bora. A family of four with two teenagers, we combined a week of ocean sailing with....*

These few sentences explain it's a family trip and describe the sailing waters where we cruised.

The third paragraph describes one's qualifications to write this article: *A lifelong, blue-water sailor, I have chartered yachts in most of the world's great cruising grounds. My articles have appeared in Yachting, Sailing World, Pacific Yachting, Sail, and other sailing publications in North America, Europe, and Australasia.*

The fourth paragraph gives personal background, such as where you live, affiliations with writers' groups, awards and professional recognitions received, and relevant educational background.

The fifth paragraph adds information, such as the types of photos you could supply, maps of the region, and an offer to include a "Travel Tips" sidebar with all the information someone needs when planning a similar trip: travel arrangements, customs requirements, land accommodations, currency exchange rates, airlines, visa information, and other details.

Even with this approach made directly to the responsible editor, you may not receive a response for quite a while. After four or five weeks, it's acceptable to send a follow-up request for a reply (not a telephone call this time). This will trigger the editor's memory to search in an undoubtedly crowded in-box to dig out a response.

Multiple Queries

The how-to books say to send only one query to one publication at a time and wait for a response before sending it to a second possibility. If you send two queries to different publications at the same time, the concern is what to do if both accept your article. However, "one at a time" is a bad strategy, because it could take months to place a piece if you have to wait through one rejection after another until your article finds a home. When I have half a dozen potential outlets for an article idea, I send queries simultaneously to them all. And if they all accept...

Hey, we want to make more money, so we can't turn down business! What kind of writer are you that you can't cover a subject from many different angles? When I get multiple acceptances, I write articles with varied slants on the same subject, thus avoiding repetitions and conflicts among publications.

Once I received assignments from two national magazines to write about a new gondola installation at one of the country's top ski resorts. For one piece I interviewed the marketing manager and slanted the story toward the benefits for skiers: time saved compared to the two chairlifts it replaced, enclosed comfort on cold and windy days, ease of riding up the mountain without wearing skis, access for sightseers, accommodation for children too small to ride a chairlift, and enhanced prestige for the ski resort.

For the other article I interviewed the gondola manufacturer and discussed the technical features: faster line speed compared with the previous chairlifts, improved safety, ability to download tired skiers, facilitation of emergency rescue, ease of maintenance, and adaptability in summer to carry equipment for bicyclists and campers.

Even with the demise of so many print publications in recent years, plenty of markets still pay top price for well-written articles. Now you know how to find them and the best way to approach them.

4
SPONSORED TRAVEL

Profitability is the difference between income and expenses. A successful business person learns to maximize the former and minimize the latter. Although this principle is simple and obvious, I'm not sure many freelancers understand it. In this chapter, I focus on expenses a freelance writer incurs. Most are minor and easy to control: utilities, office supplies, and equipment (computer, printer, and camera).

Travel Expenses

But then there's the big expense: travel. Whatever you write about, you will likely need to travel, and we all face the same problems—how to keep these expenses down. As with everything I did early in my career, I made mistakes, especially when it came to controlling these costs.

My early assignments involved writing for local boating magazines and the *Seattle Times* newspaper about sailing regattas around Puget Sound near my home in Seattle. Costs ranged from nil to minimal. I would drive to the hosting yacht club, present my press credentials, and set out for a day on the water in a launch provided by the host. It was lots of fun, and if I priced my time at zero, I made a few bucks after covering expenses for gas, parking, and lunch— essentially a breakeven proposition. Expenses were a little higher when I covered regional events and had to pay for accommodations and meals, but often I could crash with a friend and load up on snacks and drinks at the hosted cocktail hour, which would serve as dinner. So what if an assignment cost me a few hundred dollars? I was having a good time and garnering tear sheets that built creds with my editors.

But the next step was more complicated. When I started writing sailing articles for national magazines, I traveled outside the Pacific Northwest, thus adding the cost of airfare, hotels, and rental cars. I reaped psychological rewards from sailing state-of-the-art racing/cruising yachts and engaging in an activity I loved. But I never made money—or to be blunt, I forked out a lot of cash to indulge in what was more a hobby than a job. Furthermore, there was no way to handle the logistics of traveling to an offshore racing event or an international charter sailing destination.

Sponsored Travel

It took a few years to figure everything out, but I eventually learned how to arrange sponsored travel and accommodations—ways to travel any place in the world with someone else covering the costs. Soon I was receiving a dozen or so free air tickets annually, including international flights. In one 18-month period, for example, I made four trips to Europe, two to the Caribbean, and one each to Brazil, South Africa, and Croatia, as well as several domestic flights—all at no cost!

How did I do it? Airlines, hotels, resorts, and tourism businesses are willing to sponsor writers, but they must be approached in a professional manner. The travel industry operates with thin profit margins, and managers in this business focus upon the bottom-line impact in every decision. They expect anyone who works with them to understand their economic model and communicate in a businesslike fashion. When asked for support, they expect the equivalent of a mini business plan. They want to know what's being requested, how much it will cost, and how it will benefit their organization.

As a writer in search of travel support, I have to be realistic in my requests. For example, it's unlikely that I could get a free air ticket to Chicago or New

York—well-developed markets for business travelers. However, it's been easy to get complimentary first-class seats to Turkey, Tahiti, the Grenadines, and other parts of the world that are off the beaten path.

How to Contact Sponsors

Before making contact with the travel industry, I query a magazine for an assignment, typically about a charter-yacht cruising area or scuba-diving destination. Up front I stipulate that accepting the assignment is conditional upon my arranging transportation. This way, if things don't work out, I can relinquish the assignment without damaging my reputation.

With assignment in hand, I approach the airline, typically calling the media relations officer, public relations manager, or someone in sales and marketing. This process involves a lot of telephone runaround, but eventually I find the person who handles media travel. I telephone and, after telling the manager about my assignment, ask about the protocol for requesting a free ticket to a particular destination during a specific time period. I don't ask for travel support at this point, only about the process for making a request.

Sometimes the person gives an immediate response, usually negative, that they have a blackout during the time frame requested or that a certain destination is no longer open for media. Then I move on to another airline.

However, if I get a positive response, I follow up several days later with a formal request along with article links or clips and confirmation of my assignment. In my request, I give a flexible time frame that is not during peak season because I don't intend to cut into the airline's revenue stream. All I want is an airline seat that would otherwise be empty. Sometimes there can be quite a bit of back-and-forth as the airline seeks to verify the validity of my request. Eventually the request is granted.

Once I have a confirmed air ticket, I seek out the leading resort or hotel in the region and ask for its media contact, which is often a separate public relations firm. I telephone to introduce myself and discuss my assignment. After mentioning that I have received complimentary air travel, which is a strong selling point, I ask if the resort would consider hosting me for a few days during my visit. I don't press for an immediate answer. Rather, I offer to submit my request in writing along with article references and credentials. If I handle my approach professionally, the resort practically always offers complimentary accommodations.

Three nights is the maximum stay typically offered. During my early years as a freelancer, when trips lasted longer, I would check out of the elegant resort where I had been hosted and find a cheapie motel for the remaining nights, figuring that I had done the best I could.

However, on a trip to the Big Island of Hawaii, I learned another technique to arrange additional free accommodations. While I was being hosted at the Mauna Lani Resort, I called the nearby Mauna Kea Resort to request a tour. The marketing director obliged, but when he learned where I was staying, he offered me a room for a few nights at his property so I could have another taste of the local lodging facilities.

I suggested that this would perhaps be unethical to my host hotel, but he assured me that there would be no problem either for him or his counterpart back at my resort. Later I discussed this offer with my current host, and he agreed that it would be helpful for my story to learn about other lodgings in the area. Hotels and resorts often work together, recognizing that if a journalist writes about an area, everyone benefits. So I accepted the second invitation, thereby further minimizing my costs, as well as garnering more information for my articles.

After this experience, I would regularly request accommodations at two or three leading hotels on my longer trips. To keep everything aboveboard, I'd let all my hosts know that I was an invited guest with their competitors. I have never received complaints or protests about this practice. Quite the contrary, the public relations firms are often pleased that I get a well-rounded look at the region's lodging alternatives.

This approach of soliciting support from airlines, resorts, and hotels works equally well with rental car agencies, equipment suppliers, yacht-charter companies, and outdoor outfitters; ironically, you will have more success the more upscale you go. Forget the funky airlines and lower-grade accommodations. You'll never get much more than a 10 percent discount from Motel 6, Best Western, or Holiday Inn. And don't count on a free air ticket from a local airline. However, if you approach the world's leading resorts and major airlines, you might land a suite at the Four Seasons or a first-class seat on United Airlines.

Payback to Sponsors

What can your hosts expect in return? The payback can be tricky because editors often don't take kindly to blatant promotion of the sponsoring airline and resorts. On the other hand, airlines and hotels don't want a credit at the end of the article. They want to be worked into the story. They prefer that the reader feel that their services and facilities are an integral part of the adventure that I'm writing about.

Here are some typical phrasings that I've used to work my sponsors into the article. For a resort or hotel, I'd write something like, *Upon arriving in*

(Sydney/Auckland/Papeete/etc.), I checked into the (Regent Hotel/Hilton Hotel/Four Seasons Resort/etc.) to sleep off the jet lag in an elegant, relaxed setting before exploring the region's scuba-diving hot spots.

Or similarly with airlines, I might note, *As our (Qantas/Alitalia/South African Airways/etc.) jet circled over (Sydney Harbor/Naples/Cape Town, etc.), I smiled as I saw below the marina where I would pick up my charter yacht and set forth to explore some of the finest cruising waters in the world.*

Ostensibly I'm discussing recovering from jet lag or spotting the boat nestled in a marina. However, my sponsors recognize the payback, namely, that I'm referring to their hotel or overhead jet. They're happy, because I've incorporated them into the adventure of the journey.

It's important to emphasize with sponsors why supporting me helps them to reach their customers. I explain that readership for these articles consists of high net-wealth individuals who usually travel first class and stay in the world's best resorts. Once home, the travelers recount their experiences to friends who may make a similar trip. I add that I seek out other story angles during the visit, so the airline and resorts can expect additional articles on related subjects. Finally, I point out that whereas a magazine staff writer will produce only one article one time for a single publication, I, as a freelance writer, will likely place the story in several publications and will recycle the article for years to come.

Airlines are most willing to give out tickets, often first class, if they're the major carrier to a particular destination, especially when they're trying to build traffic in that market. Using this approach I have secured complimentary air travel and accommodations to New Caledonia, Fiji, Tahiti, New Zealand, Thailand, Brazil, Alaska, Northern Territories (Canada), Japan, Croatia, Marshall Islands, Belize, Costa Rica, Ecuador, Peru, Bahamas, and about a dozen trips each to Australia and the Caribbean. Once, when I had assignments first in Sydney and then shortly afterward in Naples, Qantas and Alitalia teamed up with their codeshare partners to give me a ticket around the world.

Glitches Happen

Air France had offered to comp me on a flight from Los Angeles to Papeete on a date I had requested. A week or so before that date, they called and apologized that they couldn't confirm my trip because the first-class section was booked out and asked if I could fly a couple of days later. I said I was fine with flying economy class, but they refused, insisting I could only fly first class because when they host a journalist they want to showcase the best service they offer. Thinking of the elegant French wine and gourmet food I might miss, I readily delayed my trip as they requested.

Of course, glitches will happen, and here's one that was particularly challenging. For a 1986 assignment in South Africa to report on a stopover during a single-handed sailing race around the world, South African Airways offered me a free ticket to fly from New York to Cape Town. The day I arrived in New York and was scheduled to catch the flight to Cape Town, President Reagan announced an embargo with South Africa, and the national airline immediately lost landing rights at JFK Airport. Quite apologetic, the airline spokesman said the best he could offer was a flight from London to Cape Town, but I had to make my way to England to catch the flight.

Stranded in New York, I called British Airways and, after explaining my predicament, asked for the cheapest ticket to London. I thought I would have to pay because there wasn't time to make a professional presentation of my credentials as a journalist. However, the PR representative at British Airways instead offered to give me a free ticket to London. He paused a moment and then insisted that I fly with them from London all the way to South Africa. He didn't want to share credit with a rival carrier. Another advantage, he pointed out, was British Airways could fly south from London directly over the African continent; however, South African Airways, because of embargo restrictions of air rights by a number of African countries, had to fly over the ocean around the continent, making for a much longer flight. On the return trip he added another enticement. I could fly home nonstop from London to Seattle and wouldn't get stuck again in New York. Needless to say, I immediately changed over to British Airways. (As an interesting aside, when I flew between London and Cape Town, I didn't have to reset my watch—they're in the same time zone with the same date, but six months apart in seasons.)

The only other problem I had with airlines was my fault, and I feel embarrassed whenever I think about it. I had lined up a bareboat charter yacht in New Caledonia, a French territory in the South Pacific. My story would focus on the neighboring Isle of Pines, which was once a French penal colony but now is only sparsely inhabited. Because the island was never a European settlement and was populated only by prisoners and native Caledonians, it is today considered the most natural, untouched island in the Pacific. Although excited to see the pristine beauty of the natural vegetation, I was apprehensive about sailing there because the island is encircled by treacherous coral heads and reefs, the main reason it was selected as a prison.

Although I felt certain Air France, my first choice, would give me a ticket to fly from Los Angeles to Noumea, the capital of New Caledonia, known as the Paris of the Pacific, they declined. The only other airline was Air Caledonia, which offered me a round-trip ticket. I accepted and safely completed the two-week sail to explore this unspoiled island. When I submitted the article, I had a mental lapse and mistakenly credited Air France for my flights. Although I apologized profusely, my host was understandably infuriated.

Other Benefits

Sponsored travel does more than save money. My hosts usually help access the places and people I want to see. Often the resort provides a courtesy car and driver. Other times my sponsors arrange introductions to people I need to interview for my story. Furthermore, a five-star resort provides the perfect setting for conversing with sources.

Over the years I have used variations of this approach to request sponsored travel and have practically always received support. Editors encourage my seeking hosted travel because they know I couldn't afford to incur these expenses on my own, in which case they would not get the article they had assigned. Therefore, they indulge me when I slip credits for support into my articles. Likewise airlines and my travel hosts have always been pleased, with the exception noted above, with the coverage I have given them.

Because my hosts provide an airline seat or hotel room that would otherwise be vacant, my freebie costs them nothing; yet in return they gain promotion that, if they purchased an advertisement in the magazine, would normally cost thousands of dollars.

5
PRESS TRIPS

Press trips, another form of sponsored travel, are intended to inspire journalists to promote a destination. The journeys can be organized by convention and visitor bureaus, tourism departments, public relations firms, resort chains, outfitters, or recreational enterprises such as ski areas, fishing resorts, and hunting preserves. The attraction of press trips is that everything is provided—meals, accommodations, transportation, activities, people to interview, and resource materials. You merely need to show up.

Getting Invited

Press trips are expensive to organize because the hosts, hoping all the effort will yield excellent media coverage, treat participants to the very best a destination offers. To get their money's worth, they schedule events for every minute from early morning until late at night. Breakfasts at 6 a.m. are followed by nonstop activities culminating with elegant dinners that usually include entertainment and speeches lasting well into the night...leaving only a few hours until the next 5:30 a.m. wake-up call.

The challenge with press trips is to secure an invitation. Hosts want to ensure that invited journalists will "produce"—meaning give them extensive media coverage. Even when you offer the required letter of assignment, the host may decide the publication you represent does not match the demographics or circulation numbers they want, and therefore reject you.

For a freelancer this can be a problem because often you don't know what your article will cover until you visit a place and only then discover what it offers. In cases like this, I tell the host I will find a subject or subjects to write about once I'm there, and my reputation as a professional journalist should make it unnecessary to have an assignment in advance. I also point out that as a freelancer I will produce more than one article for one publication, which is all a staff writer can guarantee. Furthermore, I will likely update and recycle the article for other publications in the years ahead. Despite these assurances, however, the organizer may select a staff writer from a national publication over a freelancer.

Get Insider Information

The digital era revolutionized the content of articles for print publications, making press trips more important than ever. Prior to the internet, editors wanted articles packed with facts and figures. For example, when writing about ski resorts I was expected to include the number of skiable acres, types of ski lifts, ticket prices, hours of operation, schedule of events, and other pertinent facts. After digging out this information from the resort's brochures and public relations materials, I would include it in my articles. Now, none of that is needed. If readers want facts, they can find everything on the resort's website.

Editors now want articles about what's *not* on the website—the insider tips. What's it like to stay at the resort? Where do you ski when visibility is poor? How do you escape the crowds? Where can you find powder stashes three days after a storm when most terrain is skied out? Writers need to cover the intangibles, the touchy-feely aspects of the experience.

The need for this type of information highlights the importance of press trips where local guides offer comprehensive tours. On your own, it would be hard to get answers to these types of questions, but press trips provide access to knowledgeable locals who have these answers and can show you places you would never find on a three-day research visit alone.

Most Significant Press Trip

The most significant press trip I ever took was in the winter of 2003 when I received a call from a ski tour organization in Oregon asking if I could immediately join one of its groups for 10 days skiing in Italy. I agreed, and two days later was at Courmayeur, a picturesque alpine village near the French border in the shadow of Mont Blanc, the highest peak in the Alps. The group included about a dozen paying guests from all over the U.S. and only one other journalist.

For the next week and a half we enjoyed perfect ski conditions there and at five nearby ski resorts. At one ski area the guide gave me a perfect lede for my article that typifies skiing in Europe. At noon he gathered the group at the summit near the Matterhorn on the Italian-Swiss border.

"What do you want for lunch today?" he asked. "Pasta" (pointing to the Italian side) "or cheese fondue?" (pointing down the Swiss slope to the village of Zermatt). All hands went up for pasta. "Then pasta, it is!" and he led the way skiing down to Cervinia.

Much as I enjoyed the skiing, the Italian food and wine, and the company of the group, my attention was increasingly diverted to Risa, a food and wine journalist from San Francisco. We stayed in touch after returning home and shared photos and notes from the trip as we prepared our articles.

When I suggested she join an upcoming press trip to Croatia, to which I had been invited, she queried the organizer about writing a food and wine article. She was quickly accepted, and a month later we met in Zagreb to begin a weeklong tour of the country. Next was a press trip to Tanzania, where I wrote about the wildlife parks and Risa covered the local foods. To avoid this becoming a love story, I'll stop here except to say a romance blossomed, and we traveled together for the next few years, and subsequently married. Ever since, we continue to find complementary assignments where I write about adventure and Risa covers food, wine, and travel.

Ethical Issues

Press trips raise more ethical issues than perhaps any other aspect of freelance writing. I follow 10 principles to avoid potential conflicts and ethical problems:

1. No Guarantees – Make it clear that although you're grateful for travel support, you can't promise or guarantee that your host will get a mention in your article. It's ethical to include the positives of support received, if deserved and relevant to the story. What's not ethical is

to promise to repay with favorable commentary. The support must be given and received unconditionally—no guarantees, no promises, and no requirements. In any case, it's the editor who has the final word about what appears in print or gets cut.

2. Editor's Approval – Prior to the trip inquire whether subsidized travel is allowed by the publication, and obtain approval from your editor for the travel support you intend to seek. After arrangements have been made, confirm the details of what's being provided with the editor.

3. No Add-on Requests – Never ask for additional amenities or activities after arriving at your destination. Prior to the trip, verify exactly what is included. If lodging is covered, are meals included as well? What about shuttle transfers and tips? Is there a fee for equipment usage? It's awkward and unethical to ask for additional services once you're on the scene.

4. Tip Generously – Regardless of what your host offers, you're still obliged to leave the customary gratuities, and perhaps a little extra, for the staff. After all, that's their livelihood, and they're not the ones who have agreed to host you.

5. Be Respectful – Be aware of local customs and honor the usual guest-host relationships.

Dress codes are important. Some airlines request that you wear business attire when they provide a first-class seat. And have the courtesy not to look like a slob if you're a guest at a five-star resort.

6. Follow the Schedule – Stick to the agreed schedule and be punctual, even if you're exhausted or don't feel like showing up for that 6 a.m. breakfast. Accept graciously and willingly whatever arrangements your host has made.

7. Be Understanding – If your host changes plans due to bad weather, equipment breakdowns, or other unforeseen circumstances, be gracious. If the planned scuba trip doesn't materialize, don't complain. Your host is as dismayed as you are.

8. No Guests – Alert your host ahead of time if you'd like to bring a guest and offer to pay the incremental costs. Children have a place only on press trips that are geared for families.

9. Send Thanks – After returning home, follow up with thank-you notes acknowledging activities, events, and helpful personnel.

10. Send Clips – When your article appears in print or online, send tear sheets, PDFs, or links. If the story is canceled, inform your hosts that you are looking for another outlet.

In any case, issue another round of thank-you notes.

Follow the Schedule

An awkward moment came up on a press trip to Mexico hosted by the Westin International hotel chain. Westin had paid all expenses, including travel to its five properties scattered throughout the country. On the last day we had half a day free in Mexico City. Just as we were leaving to tour the city on our own, one of the journalists told the group she wanted to see the new Marriott property that just opened. Whereupon our Westin hostess glared at her and said, "Don't you dare!" The rest of us were stunned that another journalist would say something that was not only stupid, but, worse yet, was a clear ethical violation.

On an African press trip that included Tanzania, the host had scheduled a 6 a.m. breakfast so we could get away early to view wildlife. As we were sitting down that morning, I noticed that one of our group was missing. Thinking she had overslept, I volunteered to rouse her. When I arrived at her tent to awaken her, she sleepily informed me she had planned to sleep late and would join us at the scheduled departure time. I practically threw her out of bed and emphasized that regardless of our preferences, as invited guests we must attend all events on the schedule.

On a Caribbean press trip sponsored by St. Kitts & Nevis Tourism, one of the journalists decided to make her own schedule and disappeared for hours at a time from our group. She missed breakfasts, was late for other meals, and lagged behind on visits to several plantation estate houses to conduct more research elsewhere on her own. When she willingly toured the elegant sugarcane-era great houses renovated for luxury guest accommodations but refused to visit the more modest, locally owned motels, it was the last straw for the tour leader, himself a native Kittitian. He ordered the journalist's belongings packed and sent to the airport, and she was off the island on the next flight. Lesson learned: don't follow your personal agenda on a press trip.

Journalistic Integrity

How do you decide whether to participate on a press trip? I have three criteria for myself: Can I get an article from it? Will expenses be covered? Can I write what I want without restrictions? If these conditions are satisfied, I will accept without regard for whoever hosts the trip. But a recent journey made me weigh decisions more carefully.

I had traveled to Israel on a press trip organized by the Ski Club of International Journalists (SCIJ) with programs underwritten by the Israeli government and several private Israeli companies. The weeklong itinerary balanced the historic (Masada, Akko, Caesarea), modern (desalination plant, wineries,

Fassuta, Tel Aviv), biblical (Jerusalem, Nazareth), political (West Bank, Golan Heights, Kibbutz Ein Gedi), and recreational (Hadera, Dead Sea).

After we returned home, controversy began. Other colleagues who did not participate on the trip attacked our group and deemed the visit unprofessional, unethical, and contrary to standards of journalistic integrity. Wow! Was I taken aback!

Why? The first criticism was that the itinerary included a visit to the Golan Heights, territory in Syria that was captured by Israel in 1967. When annexed by Israel in 1981, the UN Security Council said the action violated the Fourth Geneva Convention prohibiting acquisition of territory by force. Our itinerary included presentations at the Golan Winery by Israelis living in the settlement of Katzrin. International law regards the Israelis living there as illegal settlers.

The second criticism was that we participating journalists compromised the integrity of SCIJ by visiting territory that Israel occupies. Critics asserted we were unwittingly used as public relations tools. While in the Golan Heights, settlers, and most likely government agents traveling incognito, photographed us enjoying ourselves and commenting on the excellent wine, as though this was all part of Israel.

The third criticism was the suggestion that after being feted on an excursion paid for in part by the Israeli government, we would be unlikely to write anything negative about our experience.

After reflecting on these criticisms, I rejected all three. This trip was about journalistic research and I needed to be there, regardless of the circumstances, for the firsthand experience. How else could I interview UN peacekeepers from Australia stationed at the contested border with Syria, where I heard continuous gunfire of ISIS troops? And where else other than at Israel's southernmost city of Eilat on the Red Sea could I view the shorelines of three Arab countries? Egypt and Jordan were visible less than a quarter mile away while the hazy outline of Saudi Arabia loomed just 12 miles distant. Only then did I understand why militaries of all countries are on constant alert.

And how else could I have found a quote that sums up the complexity of the region as succinctly as that from Michael Asi, a Greek Orthodox priest in the Palestinian Christian village of Fassuta in northern Israel, which is subject to frequent shelling by the nearby guns from Lebanon: *"We are Israeli but not Jewish, Arab but not Muslim, Catholic but not Roman Catholic."*?

Bottom line:

- I'm glad I went on this research trip, which I could never otherwise afford as a freelance writer;

- Regardless of the occupied land issue, I got firsthand information about the Golan Heights;

- My articles are balanced and explain political controversies.

OOPS!

I have been caught up in awkward situations on occasion. Few people know that part of the Amazon River flows through Ecuador, which claims more rivers per square mile than any other country. On a press trip sponsored by the Ecuadorian Ministry of Tourism, I spent a week in the jungle with indigenous people, paddling among native villages to research their tourism offerings and to photograph native fauna, flora, and people. At the end of the trip, I had everything needed for my article. But shortly after my return home, two American oil workers were killed by tribal people protesting oil drilling in their pristine rainforest territory.

My editor immediately canceled the story on the grounds that she could not encourage tourists to visit Ecuador under these risky circumstances. Despite my best efforts I never found a home for the article, much to the consternation of my host.

Another time I had a boating magazine assignment to cover how experienced sailors can participate in sailing a square-rigged tall ship. I set off on a one-week cruise, ready to climb the ratlines, hang from the yardarms, balance on the footropes, and unfurl the sails. Donning proper boat shoes and sailing gloves on the first morning at sea, I joined the professional crew on deck, ready to lend a hand. That's when I was informed that for liability reasons, passengers could not help operate the vessel. Since I hadn't completely researched the way the trip would run, the article had to be scuttled. One would think that in an industry built upon the proper use of words, misunderstandings such as this could not occur. They do, although thankfully not too often.

The bottom line: when participating on a press trip, make sure that every detail is clarified in advance. Such journeys are wonderful resources for freelancers, but if things go wrong, blame will fall on the writer, who will likely never again work for the assigning editor and never again be invited on another press trip by that same host.

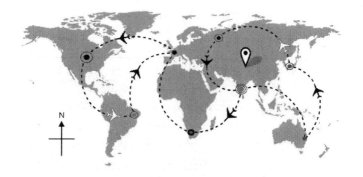

6
LEVERAGED GLOBE-TROTTING

Because travel expenses can take such a large chunk of a freelance writer's budget, it's worth another chapter to discuss ways to defray these costs.

Frequent-Flyer Programs

In addition to arranging sponsored travel and press trips, there's another approach to minimize travel expenses: leveraging airline frequent-flyer programs. Airlines create these programs to build brand loyalty by rewarding travelers with bonus tickets if they fly a certain number of miles. But you don't ever have to buy an airline ticket to earn these mileage awards. At one time I had more than 200,000 frequent-flyer miles available to redeem air tickets, none of which were earned by paying for an airline ticket!

Let's look at how these frequent-flyer programs, also called affinity programs or loyalty programs, work. Every airline offers frequent-flyer awards in partnership with other domestic and international carriers, and memberships are free. In addition, every airline allows you to buy, share, and transfer miles. Although programs vary depending upon time of year and other considerations, a round-trip domestic flight typically requires 20,000 to 25,000 frequent-flyer miles, and a foreign destination needs 30,000 to 50,000. Several airlines offer one-way tickets for domestic flights for only 5,000 miles. Rules are complex, but once you understand them, you can use miles not only for free flights and upgrades, but also for discounts on hotel accommodations, restaurant meals, car rentals, ship cruises, vacations, magazines, and other purchases.

The first step, which is free, is to join the frequent-flyer programs of all the major domestic airlines: Alaska Airlines Mileage Plan, American Airlines AAdvantage Program, Delta Air Lines SkyMiles Program, Southwest Airlines Rapid Rewards Program, and United Airlines MileagePlus Program. Although the plans are similar, occasionally you'll find a unique feature that may be important to you. For example, if you buy a lot of wine, you may be interested in Alaska Airlines' "Wine-Flies-Free" program that allows Mileage Plan members to ship a case of wine without it counting against the checked baggage allowance.

Airline Credit Cards

Every airline issues one or more credit cards, and they are the key to leveraging the frequent-flyer programs. Therefore, the second step is to get a credit card from each of these airlines and avail yourself of the bonus introductory miles they offer. Although the provisions and terms were valid at the time of this writing, incentives to sign up for these credit cards change frequently, but tend to stay in the ballpark noted below.

Alaska's Signature Visa card — Awards 40,000 bonus miles plus a $99 companion fare ticket if you spend $2,000 within the first 90 days of opening the account. Your first bag is checked free as well as those for up to six guests. You can also apply for Alaska's Business Visa card and receive an additional 40,000 bonus miles plus a companion certificate after spending $2,000 in the first 90 days. Annual fees are $75 for each card. With Alaska's lowest one-way fares available for only 5,000 miles, right away you have enough miles for several round-trip domestic tickets.

American's AAdvantage Premium Select World Elite MasterCard — Awards 50,000 miles after spending $2,500 within three months of opening, and the $99 annual fee is waived the first year. This mileage allowance is sufficient for two round-trip domestic tickets. Another American credit card, the AAdvantage Aviator World MasterCard offers 60,000 miles, the first bag checked free, and a $99 companion certificate if the first purchase is made within 90 days. For business owners (as a freelance writer you qualify as a sole proprietorship business) American offers the CitiBusiness Platinum Select card that awards 65,000 bonus miles and waives the $99 annual fee the first year if you spend $4,000 in the first four months. These miles combined are more than sufficient for an international round-trip ticket on American or one of its partners.

Delta's SkyMiles Gold American Express Card — Awards 40,000 bonus miles, first bag checked free, and the $99 fee waived the first year if you spend $1,000 the first month. For business owners, the corresponding SkyMiles Gold Business American Express card offers 40,000 miles if you spend $2,000 in the first three months.

Hawaiian's MasterCard — Offers 70,000 miles plus a 50 percent companion discount if you spend $2,000 in the first three months, enough for a round trip from the mainland to Hawaii. The Hawaiian Airlines Business MasterCard awards 60,000 miles upon spending $1,000 in the first 90 days and an additional 10,000 miles after first use by a second employee. Both cards charge an annual fee of $99.

Southwest's Visa Signature Card — Offers 40,000 Rapid Reward points after spending $1,000 within three months after applying. Annual membership is $69. Depending upon the destination, these points could be sufficient for up to 10 one-way segments. Southwest's business card offers 80,000 points after spending $5,000 within 90 days and 9,000 points on each anniversary date. The annual fee is $199.

United's MileagePlus Explorer Visa Card — Comes with 60,000 miles and waives the $95 annual fee the first year if you spend $3,000 in the first three months. You get an additional 10,000 miles if you spend in total $6,000 within six months. The United Business Card offers 75,000 miles after spending $5,000 within three months.

By acquiring the credit cards from these six airlines, you'll have enough free travel opportunities to make multiple trips anywhere in the country and several trips abroad. If you pick up the business cards as well, you will have sufficient miles to last several years. However, there's even more you can do to earn additional award miles once you have the credit cards.

The goal of each airline with its frequent-flyer program is to encourage participants to accumulate award tickets by purchasing an air ticket and earning one award mile for every mile flown. But that's cumbersome, slow, and expensive. You have to purchase about a dozen air tickets to earn one free domestic economy-class flight. In any case, because in the future you won't need to buy an air ticket, you won't accrue any points in this manner anyway. But you can earn miles to leverage the mileage programs without flying—and it's much quicker.

Pick Your Primary Airlines

Once you have a cluster of credit cards in hand and have received the new card member bonuses, feel free to set the cards aside. You're under no obligations to use them ever again. You get the sign-up bonuses and the special-promotion benefits once you've met the purchase requirements. They're not rescinded if you don't use them.

When deciding upon a primary frequent-flyer program, pick an airline that serves your hometown with routes to your usual destinations and with features important to your travel needs. If you tend to fly at the last minute, avoid airlines that charge a fee for late booking. If you vary your schedule frequently, choose airlines such as Southwest that don't charge change fees. Be aware of airlines that charge higher prices if you can't stay over on a Saturday. If you often stop over while enroute, check which airlines allow this practice. As you learn the policies of the various airlines, you'll soon figure out the ones that suit your travel plans best.

Charge Everything

In addition to using credit cards to earn maximum mileage, you can use them to manage your household and business expenses more efficiently. Charge everything—that means everything—to your card. Use it at the grocery store, gas station, movie theater, doctor's office, and post office. Purchasing a cup of coffee or a small sundry item for a few dollars? Put it on your card. Tips are practically the only reason to ever carry cash.

The only cash I carry in my wallet is what I call my pet $20 bill, and I try to keep it for as long as possible, sometimes for months, before I have to spend it. Even after I break it into change, another several weeks may pass before I use it up and am back at the ATM for another bill.

Charge to your credit cards the regular monthly bills such as cable TV, telephone, cell phone, internet, newspaper and magazine subscriptions, water, sewage, electricity, gas, heating fuel, and insurance premiums. Often you can set up these monthly charges for automatic deductions, thereby saving the hassle of writing monthly checks and making individual payments for each of these services. Contributions to charities and nonprofit organizations, including foundations, universities, hospitals, and other associations, can often be made by credit card.

Special Offers

Pay attention to special credit card offers that come up from time to time. You may be able to double the miles for a limited period for a specific category of charges such as restaurants, gas, groceries, etc. Sometimes hitting a dollar quota by a certain date will double the points for that period. Purchases from computer stores often carry bonus points. If you use the credit cards judiciously, you'll discover other paybacks such as first-class upgrades, companion tickets, discount coupons, and additional benefits.

You can also earn miles on credit cards about to expire. If a year has passed and you are billed for the annual fee, which was waived the first year, you have several ways to avoid paying it. Call to say you want to cancel the card. You'll be transferred to a separate department whose job is to get you to change your mind. You may be offered a retention benefit such as several thousand bonus miles, executive club passes, drink coupons, upgrade certificates, or another waiver of the annual fee. If this doesn't work, cancel the card and then reapply for it after a few months. Chances are, you'll once again get the bonus miles as a new cardholder. If you're uncomfortable doing this, reapply by phone and explain that you were a previous cardholder but want to apply again if you can receive the first-time benefits.

While it's not difficult to get both a consumer and a business card from the same airline, it's also possible to get bonuses as a new member multiple times with multiple consumer cards by explaining you want one card for travel costs and another for home expenses or perhaps a third card for dining charges. Customer service reps often quickly agree because many retail bank employees are evaluated by how many credit cards they issue.

Several airlines offer attractive incentives if you hit certain year-end targets. If you spend $25,000 dollars on Delta's American Express card, you'll receive an extra 10,000 bonus miles. American and United have similar enticements. If you charge $125,000 on Southwest's Rapid Rewards Visa card or otherwise earn 125,000 Rapid Rewards points within one year, you'll receive a companion pass for free travel for a year on every—yes, every—trip you take. And you can select up to three people as companions. Upon reaching a certain level, Alaska offers members elite status, which entitles them to elevated benefits and services.

If you have a family, you have even more opportunities to earn bonus miles. Your spouse and children can join the airline loyalty programs and apply for credit cards in their own names, even if they are youngsters, as long as they can claim an income that qualifies. Delta will award bonus miles on each of up to two additional cards on a business account. Get separate cards for every family member, and then sign each other up on all the business cards for additional miles.

Most rental car companies and major hotel chains offer mileage awards, many with double-mile bonuses. More than 10,000 restaurants nationwide offer between five and 10 miles for each dollar spent when you pay for your meal with a registered credit card. United Airlines offers five miles per dollar at hundreds of participating boutique hotels and resorts around the country—intimate, independent hotels that never before featured Mileage Plus miles. Throughout the summer many hotels offer double miles. It pays to ask about mileage programs at any hotel or restaurant you visit.

Airlines will often award mileage adjustments as a goodwill gesture for an inconvenience or problem incurred on a flight. I have availed myself of these offerings on occasions when they overlooked my preordered vegetarian meal, rerouted me due to a flight cancellation, or lost my luggage.

You can earn award miles if you register for email newsletters, updates, online mileage-plan statements, and special offers. Although it's a pain to deal with these email subscriptions, you can often pick up 1,000 award miles if you agree to receive these promo offerings. Of course, shortly after you receive the bonus miles and have subscribed for a reasonable period of time, you can cancel. This clears the way to sign up again at a later time.

Numerous other purchase programs offer award miles. Flowers purchased from Flowers.com and FTD earn 500 base miles plus five or 10 miles for each dollar spent. Many magazine subscription purchases have mileage awards as an incentive. You can sometimes earn miles by charging to your credit card the payments on a home mortgage, investment programs, and financial services. I've learned to inquire about airline mileage benefits whenever I engage in any commercial transaction. It's surprising how often I find programs where I least expect them.

The dollars put on your credit card add up quickly to several thousand miles each month, particularly if you're in a double-mile program. In addition, you're exercising good cash management and using your cash flow more efficiently by making a purchase today but not paying for it for four to six weeks at the conclusion of your billing cycle. Furthermore, you have a complete record for business, tax, and reference purposes for every dollar you spend.

But there's a caveat: don't ever, ever carry balances on your cards. You'll be paying interest charges around 20 percent annually. If you can't pay your credit-card bills, stop using the cards. Alternatively, when interest rates are low, refinance you home or car to access the cash you need to avoid credit-card balances.

Ethics and Rules

The issue of ethics is ever-present when leveraging mileage-award programs. I pay close attention to the rules for award promotions, although if I accidentally step over the line, the airline quickly points out the misunderstanding. I always advise the airline of what I'm doing when I respond to a promotion. For example, when I already have a particular credit card and apply for a second card to earn additional miles, I tell the customer service representative what I'm doing. Therefore, if I'm later questioned about why I have multiple credit cards, or why I canceled and later reapplied for a card, I can refer to earlier conversations in which I stated my intentions.

I'm often surprised that my approach is out of phase with, and sometimes contrary to, the approach of other freelance writers who often try to pay their own travel expenses or ask their publication for reimbursement. But the methods I describe work for me, allowing me to travel any place in the world for free (or almost). Much of the information given above may become dated with the passage of time; however, frequent-flyer programs and credit card offerings will be around for as long as the issuing airlines and banks remain in business, so check out the details for yourself.

In closing, I want to pay tribute to Christopher Columbus as a freelance writer and explorer who figured out how to nail his travel expenses. When he set out, he wasn't sure where he was going. He was mistaken about the place where he landed. And when he returned home, he still had no idea where he had been. Yet his chronicles transformed the world...and earned him two more trips to write more reports.

Best of all, he did all his travels with someone else's money!

7
PHOTOS

To be financially successful in freelance writing, you don't leave money on the table. That, however, is exactly what you do if you don't take your own · photos.

Early Mistakes

During my years as boating editor for the *Seattle Times*, the newspaper's policy required that for any assignment within 100 miles of Seattle, the images had to be taken by one of the paper's photographers. Therefore, a staff photographer tagged along to the local racing regattas I covered. We'd spend one or more enjoyable days on the water, during which time I would point out the key boats and skippers to be photographed. After we returned home, I would start writing my story, but the photographer was already done. Yet he or she earned as much as I did, even though the work of writing took days longer. Moreover, these photographers were not sailors and often had no idea what they were shooting. When I pointed out an interesting keel design or a new type of spinnaker, they often didn't understand the unique features that needed to be captured in a photograph.

There were other problems as well. Sometimes a photographer wasn't available when I needed one but came to the venue the following day when the event was over and could photograph only the deserted facilities. When my article was published, the accompanying images often bore no relation to the highlights I noted. Other times I needed photos taken on board, and the photographer, who may have never been on a sailboat before, became a seasick liability. If I was sailing with friends, the otherwise jovial atmosphere could be strained when a clumsy landlubber joined us.

At the time I thought of myself as strictly a writer. My early freelance articles on boating, scuba diving, and snow skiing were always published with someone else's photos, even though there might be little relationship between those images and the story I was telling. In other instances when the editor did not assign a photographer to cover my article, the publication used generic landscapes that failed to enhance or explain the subject matter.

Increase Income

I soon realized that with a little training I could take my own photos. I signed up for photography courses and purchased Nikon gear. Because publications pay for writing and photos separately, I saw my income immediately increase by 50 to 100 percent. Equally important, I had control over the photos that accompanied my articles and could highlight points in the text with specific images.

I also got more acceptances with my queries when I told editors I could provide images with the article. Editors appreciate getting complete packages of text and images because it makes their job easier: they don't need to find photos to accompany an article. Even if the writing is weak, it may be accepted if the photos are strong and vice versa. Editors sometimes respond to a query by asking first to see the photos and then make a decision to accept or reject.

A further bonus is that on some press trips, my writing colleagues sought photos to accompany their articles and I could offer whatever they needed. Naturally I wanted the photo credit, but to make the deal more attractive and prevent them from working with another photographer, I would offer them a percentage of the payment I received.

As additional enhancement ·of my income, I sometimes made sales of images alone. An editor of a sailing magazine asked to use an image of a classical sailing yacht for a sales-promotion piece. Payment received was comparable to a 350-word article. When the South African editor of *South Africa Yachting* magazine, for which I was the longtime North American editor, asked to use an image of one of the country's famous single-handed sailors for the magazine cover, I was surprised that the fee exceeded the amount I received for writing the magazine's lead feature article. (During the apartheid era when South African rands could not be sent out of the country, I gladly received cases of the country's wine in payment.)

Problems

Combining writing and photography sometimes causes problems on press trips. If the trip is designed for writers, the writers complain if I stop the group to take photographs as we tour. If the trip is designed for photographers, we move along at a different pace—waiting for that cloud to pass or sunset colors to peak—and, as a writer, I lose opportunities for conducting interviews or researching local information.

When new to photography, I sometimes found myself out of place with other photographers. On a photo press boat in Australia's Whitsunday Islands covering a sailing regatta, I was one of a dozen photographers jammed along the railing of a motor yacht, taking photos of a racing fleet. At a certain moment I saw a photo opportunity just at the edge of my view, prompting me to lean out on the railing to get a clear shot. Suddenly a dozen shouts rose in unison, telling me to fall back in line because I was blocking the view.

On another occasion on a press trip to St. Barts in the Caribbean I watched a photographer meticulously set up for a shot looking from the beach toward the sea. First, he found a rake and cleared seaweed from a section of beach. Then he smoothed the sand and sprinkled water so it glistened in the sun. After bringing over a beach chair and tilting it back at exactly the angle he wanted, he directed a female model, who had been hired to join us for the week, to pose on the chaise longue. Setting up his tripod and camera mounting, he then began to fuss with camera lenses and filters while taking meter readings of the ambient light.

Just then another photographer, fortunately not I, stepped in and snapped the scene being set up. Whereupon the first photographer stopped what he was doing and stormed over to the interloper to inform him that if he ever saw that photo in print, he would sue him for everything he was worth. He then turned to the rest of us and asked that we serve as witnesses, if needed, to what had just happened. Although not illegal, the opportunist's action was clearly a breach of the unwritten code.

On a press trip for photographers to Belize one of our group spotted a peasant farmer tilling his land high on a distant hill. Thinking it was a worthy image, he made the shot. Even though the farmer was far away, his face was still recognizable, so the photographer, in accordance with the policy of his publication, had to secure a signed photo release. After trudging up the hill he presented the form to the non-English-speaking farmer, who shook his head, signifying a definite "No." From the van below on the road we saw vigorous gestures, with no appearance of settling the issue. A few minutes later, the photographer pulled a couple of dollar bills from his wallet. The farmer quickly signed, grabbed the offering, and resumed plowing. Moral: check if your publication requires photo releases. If it's a problem, make sure the face is not recognizable.

My biggest-ever sale of a single image was of the sailing ship *Sea Cloud*, snapped when I was on a press trip cruising in the Caribbean. The yacht previously belonged to Marjorie Merriweather Post, heiress to the Post Cereal fortune and builder of Mar-a-Lago (yes, the same property subsequently purchased by Donald Trump) in Palm Beach, Florida.

Today *Sea Cloud* operates as a luxury cruise ship. On a sunny day in perfect weather when all 29 sails were set, I launched a skiff and, while encircling the vessel, took dozens of images. Although many photos were incorporated into my articles, the biggest sale came when a book publisher asked to buy one for the cover of a children's book about tall ships. When asked the price, I said $750 for a one-time use, a fee he quickly accepted. Several years later the publisher released a second edition and again wanted rights to use the same photo for the cover. I quoted $875 and again he paid. When the third edition came out, the price increased to $1,100. I'm still waiting for the fourth edition.

I sometimes worry about a potential problem that fortunately has never come up. When an editor requests a photo of me to accompany an article, I hesitate to ask one of the pros, because he or she has claim to the photo credit and the money. To avoid this problem, I usually set up the shot and then ask a bystander to push the button. But then who gets the credit for the shot and who gets the money? It wouldn't make sense to say I took the picture because I'm in it. Not knowing what to do, I tell the editor the image is provided by me. This apparently avoids further discussion, and I receive the check.

Other Photo Sources

Even if you don't take your own photos, there are other ways of getting free images and avoiding the expense of a professional photographer. Any place you write about is likely to have a photo gallery where media can download images at no cost. Ski resorts, hunting lodges, fishing camps, convention and visitors bureaus, tourism departments, public relations firms, and other promotional organizations provide free images for media purposes, but look out for two problems. Sometimes the photos you receive are imprinted with the name of the photographer, which means your editor may have to include attribution and possibly be obliged to make a payment. Before using an image make sure there is no need for attribution or payment. Another problem might occur when the copyright symbol or a watermark is on the image, which means the editor must go through the hassle of obtaining a release. The people and places you write about should understand it is in their best interests to remove whatever stumbling blocks they impose upon the editor.

Sometimes an article works best with graphics or illustrations, and these are easily downloadable from the internet. Search for free clip art, and you'll find dozens of sites with gallery indices for whatever you're seeking: animals, birds, sea creatures, art, trees, architecture, cartoons, and more.

Although I am often dismissed as an amateur photographer by professionals, I get my share of images published and typically increase my writing income by providing photos. I don't know much about the intricacies of camera settings, but cameras today automatically adjust the time exposure and lens aperture. All I need to do is compose the image and let the camera's computers do the rest. Even when a photographer is assigned to me, I always take my camera on trips. Often the editor prefers my images to those of the pro.

So the tip is clear: take your own photos.

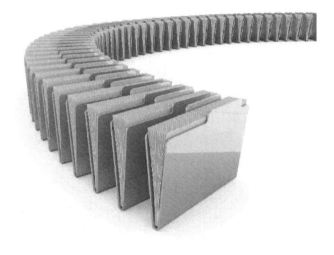

8
MULTIPLE ASSIGNMENTS

Even with complimentary travel and accommodations, it's almost impossible to make a decent wage when on a trip with only a single assignment. Including travel time, it takes a full day to cover an event such as a downhill-skiing competition or a sailing regatta. If the competition continues over a weekend or longer, I incur additional expenses for accommodations, local transportation, incidentals, and meals. Once at home I spend another day or so sorting my notes to write the article and selecting photos to submit. A publication may pay a few hundred dollars for the text and images, so the hourly rate becomes miniscule. Furthermore, the notes and images are unique to that event and immediately become outdated. Since I can't reuse them, I may as well discard them. All of this represents a lot of effort resulting in very little compensation.

Hobby or Business?

I originally justified this inefficient use of time in two ways. First, I derived a lot of pleasure hanging around the venues, meeting the contestants, and joining in the festivities with good music, plentiful food, and sponsors' gifts of T-shirts, beer mugs, and associated accessories. For example, at a sailing event sponsored by Duracell Corporation, I received a year's worth of batteries. In addition, I was building a reputation as a competent journalist, which opened doors for future writing and photo assignments.

But the lack of profitability continued to be a problem. Was I just pursuing an expensive hobby, or was I determined to make money as a freelance journalist? Because I was serious about earning a living from this work, I had to find a better way. Again, I turned to the how-to books, but again, they didn't help. They talked about getting assignments and submitting articles to publications but ignored how to build a business.

Multiple Articles

I soon realized that when I travel on what I'll call the primary assignment, I need to create a secondary assignment on a different subject, and, if possible, a third or even more. The first time I tried this approach, it worked well. Thanks to a free air ticket, I was in Brazil at the coastal city of Buzios, covering the Women's World Sailing Championships for Sail Magazine, when I saw a boat builder constructing a 15-foot fishing skiff.

With the help of a translator, I learned this traditional Brazilian design is called a jangada. Rigged for a single triangular sail, it can handle harsh conditions in the Atlantic Ocean, but it operates in a unique way. In the morning, motor yachts tow a dozen or so of these skiffs, each with a single fisherman, 30 or more miles off the coast to the continent's outer fishing banks and leave them until sunset when they return to bring them back to shore. During the intervening 12 hours at sea, these small boats are on their own to handle unexpected weather conditions. There's a danger that if they become spread out, the mother vessel may not find them at the end of the day. With camera firing away, I captured every angle of both builder and boat, thereby getting everything necessary to write a second article from that single trip to Buzios, Brazil.

But opportunities for articles from that trip weren't limited to only two. Representing 21 nations, the top female sailors who competed afforded potential as individual subjects for additional articles with no conflict with my primary assignment, which was to focus on the races themselves. I interviewed these world-class female sailors on shore and photographed them during the races, giving me everything necessary to write profiles on each. Once back home, I contacted the editors of each country's leading sailing publications and secured every assignment I queried. What a bonanza this turned out to be! I probably got close to 25 articles published. Because my air tickets and accommodations were provided free, my costs were nominal. Now I was beginning to see how to make money at freelancing.

I adapted a similar approach when I covered the BOC Challenge, one of the first single-handed sailing races around the world. The sponsor, British Oxygen Corporation, was a multinational British-based industrial-gas company that sponsored four similar global sailing challenges in subsequent years. The race started and ended in Newport, Rhode Island, with stopovers in Cape Town, Sydney, and Rio de Janeiro. Thanks to support from airlines, I was present at the start and finish of the race, as well as at each stopover where I interviewed the skippers and photographed them and their boats.

Because the race was new and not well publicized, I was the only journalist who met the boats at each stopover, which meant I got exclusive stories along the way. The winner of the 16 boats from seven countries finished after four months, while the last competitor finally crossed the finish line three months later. With editors of the sailing magazines in the seven countries interested in coverage from start to finish, I sold more than 30 articles. Comps from airlines and resorts at each stopover minimized my personal expenses, and I netted another bonanza with my articles and photos.

An interesting sidenote taught me not to be too greedy. The stopover in Sydney coincided with the America's Cup regatta at the other side of the country at Fremantle, and I thought I saw an opportunity for additional assignments covering the match races between Dennis Conner's *Stars & Stripes* and the Australian defender *Kookaburra*. Thanks to Qantas Airways, I got a free flight across the country, expecting to research an article covering the competition that would be accepted by a U.S. magazine.

Imagine my surprise when I arrived in Fremantle and found 2,500 journalists from around the world digging into every story angle imaginable. Not only were the world's major boating magazines represented, but their correspondents, who were all on expense accounts, booked the best accommodations, ate at the finest restaurants, rented private chase boats and helicopters to follow the racing, hired local staff to assist with research, and had priority in interviewing the skippers and crew. There was no place for a guy like me on a shoestring budget without an assignment. I left after a day.

Avoid National Publications

Having succeeded with two international assignments, I felt there must be a way to secure multiple assignments when writing about domestic subjects. I came up with a technique that once again contradicted the guidance in the how-to books. They encourage writers to aspire to the top-paying, prestigious national publications, but this is the wrong approach.

When I write about boating, scuba diving, or skiing for a national magazine such as *Yachting*, *Scuba Diver*, or *Skiing*, I'll receive top dollar for the story and photos plus recognition. Unfortunately national publications want first North American Rights, exclusive rights, reprint rights, and other rights to the article and photos that prevent further use. Regional publications, on the other hand, typically want only readership rights, meaning you can resell to another publication as long as it's not in their circulation area. For example, *Northwest Yachting* in Seattle, with circulation limited to the Pacific Northwest, will not pay as much for an article as *Boating Magazine*, which has national distribution. However, if, in addition to *Northwest Yachting*, I simultaneously sell the article to *Southern Boating* in Florida, the combined payment will likely exceed compensation from the national magazine.

If I add publications such as San Diego's *The Log Newspaper*, *New England Boating*, *MidWest Outdoors*, *Great Lakes Boating*, and other regional boating publications, I'll be better off financially than if I limited my sale to one national publication. The only restriction is the subject must have national or international appeal to sell in these several markets. Don't expect a Florida editor to pick up a story specific to the Pacific Northwest. Furthermore, I may have to change the lede to appeal to the local readership in each region, but then, after pasting the same body of the article, I'm finished. Regional publications proliferate in the American media landscape, so whatever subject you write about, you'll find half a dozen or more that want only readership rights, leaving you free to sell your articles to multiple publications.

If you are keen to write for national outlets and want to place your article in a second publication as well, you can do so, but your articles must differ significantly from each other, or you will likely never write for either publication again. It's not just a matter of making cosmetic adjustments. You must alter the entire slant of the piece. Examples of acceptable alterations are first person and third person, present tense and past tense, feature article and news piece. But be careful.

Professional Organizations

To broaden my scope of article ideas and publications, I join writers' organizations, of which there are more than 75 in North America, divided into a dozen categories. The two major benefits are their newsletters and annual conferences. Newsletters, which tend to be monthly or bimonthly, are packed with information about editors seeking writers, press trip hosts recruiting participants, writers looking for assignments, book publishers wanting authors, job opportunities, and tips for craft improvement. Conferences offer programs with professional development seminars, roundtable discussions, nationally acclaimed guest speakers, and opportunities to meet editors who discuss the types of articles and photographs they are seeking. Conference hosts usually showcase their local attractions by organizing a breakout day for participants to engage in activities (fishing, biking, hunting, dining, canoeing, and more) or visit sites of historical and cultural interest. Perhaps most important are opportunities to network with other professionals.

More than 25 writers organizations specialize in outdoor recreation alone. Some are regional such as Northwest Outdoor Writers Association (NOWA), which rotates conferences among the five states of its area. Locales range from a wine region in southern Oregon to a ranch in Montana. Several larger states have their own groups, including Texas Outdoor Writers Association (TOWA) and Outdoor Writers Association of California (OWAC). Other organizations are national, including Outdoor Writers Association of America (OWAA) and Professional Outdoor Media Association (POMA).

Prominent in the travel category are International Food, Wine and Travel Writers Association (IFWTWA) and Society of American Travel Writers

(SATW), both of which host conferences in the U.S. and abroad. For winter sports journalists, North American Snowsports Journalists Association (NASJA) hosts conferences at major U.S. ski resorts, and Ski Club of International Journalists (SCIJ) offers opportunities to mix with an international crowd at ski resorts around the world. Some organizations have their annual meetings at the same location every year. For example, Boating Writers International (BWI) often holds its major annual gathering at the Miami Boat Show, one of the country's largest boat exhibitions. The Society of International Nautical Scribes (SINS) is, as the name suggests, a less formal organization, and organizes conferences in conjunction with major international sailing regattas.

Foreign Markets

Another technique for finding multiple assignments is to approach foreign markets. There are seven major English-speaking nations (U.S., Canada, United Kingdom, Ireland, Australia, New Zealand, and South Africa) that produce the same types of publications as in the U.S. If your subject has international appeal, you should be able to place your article and photos in a publication in each country. In addition, a number of countries, including Mexico, Japan, and China, publish English-language magazines and newspapers that accept freelance submissions. Be careful when submitting to Canada and the U.S., as well as Ireland and the United

Kingdom, because there is likely to be an overlap of readership.

If you can develop personal relations with editors of foreign-language publications, you may find another interesting market. For example, I write for the Italian sailing magazine *Giornale della Vela* and the German boating magazines *Das Boot* and *Segeln*, as well as publications in Japan, Norway, Sweden, and Denmark. In each case I submit articles in English, which they translate into their own language. Therefore they have the advantage of putting my article into the style they prefer, while I enjoy the benefit of not struggling with their language.

How can you learn about these foreign publications? Before traveling to a new country I google its magazines that relate to the subjects I cover. Then, upon arrival, I go to a newsstand and pick up all the magazines that relate to my writing interests. Next, I telephone each editor, and, after introducing myself as an American journalist who has come to pursue a writing interest (sailing, scuba, snow skiing) in the country, ask if I can come by their offices. Although the editors have undoubtedly covered these subjects in their publications, I often nail down additional assignments by asking if they would like an American perspective on their cruising grounds or dive sites or ski resorts. This new relationship often leads to additional assignments in the future.

Today I have overseas markets for my articles and photos in most European countries, in Australasia, and in several island-nations in the South Pacific and the Caribbean. Furthermore, because I have a good rapport with the editors of these publications, I can send queries and be relatively assured of timely, personal responses.

Likewise, when I travel throughout the U.S. I seek new contacts at regional publications. This gives me access to small publications that, although they don't pay much, are a good market for reprints.

The takeaway tips: never take on an assignment unless you can get at least three article placements, avoid national publications in favor of regional outlets with no overlapping readerships, and develop markets abroad.

9
NEWSPAPERS

Freelance writers have to approach newspapers differently from how they work with magazines. Because newspapers typically pay only several hundred dollars for an article with no allowance for expenses, you have to ensure travel expenses are nominal to make the assignment financially worthwhile. Write for a newspaper only if covering a local event near your home to avoid accommodation expenses, or if the article can be written in connection with another well-paying assignment while you're on the road with travel expenses covered.

I have worked with newspapers in three different ways.

Local Multi-Day Events

As boating editor for the *Seattle Times*, despite the fancy title, I was just a stringer paid at most a few hundred dollars for 500-word news articles reporting results of local sailing regattas. Low pay, lots of fun, and I handled my own expenses.

A one-day event never makes sense financially, but if an event lasts a three-day weekend and the assignment is for three articles, I would accept. The downside is the tight deadline to submit the article by 11 p.m. in time for the next day's paper. At the end of the day when everyone is celebrating in the bar, I miss the fun while holing up in a quiet room for a few hours to write the article. I finish about the time the bar closes and the food is gone.

If traveling for another purpose, I look for local events wherever I go. A visit to New York City for personal reasons coincided with the Six Metre World Cup at Seawanhaka Yacht Club on Centre Island at Oyster Bay, Long Island. The editor of the local newspaper, hearing I was in town, asked that I write a daily column during the six-day event. When she offered accommodations in her stately home on the bay as well as fair payment for the articles and photos, I readily accepted.

I was excited to be part of this event, because Seawanhaka and the Six Metre yacht, which competed for many years in the Olympics, are two of the most prestigious names in yacht racing. I had a great time and my articles were well received. As a side benefit, I sold many racing photos of individual boats to the skippers and crew. Best of all, the International Six Metre Association committee was so impressed with my coverage that it arranged for me to travel to Sweden two years later to cover the next World Cup on the island of Sandhamn in the Stockholm Archipelago. Who knows where things can lead?

Hometown Articles

Hometown newspaper articles are about newsworthy events of individuals or groups from that locale. On one occasion I had been invited to join a tour on a small cruise ship for a 10-day round-trip voyage from Seattle to Anchorage with stops at towns and attractions in Alaska along the way. A few days prior to the ship arriving at a well-known glacier, a young couple from Ohio decided this would be the perfect venue to get married. The tour host arranged the wedding license and found an officiant; meanwhile, the couple asked me to be a witness.

After anchoring on the appointed day, the captain took us ashore in the launch and we scrambled to the top of the glacier. Decked out in our best fleece and parkas, we celebrated the ceremony with eagles flying overhead and the booming sounds of the calving glacier below us. After the trip I transcribed my notes and sent off 300 words with photos to the couple's hometown newspaper. Some days later the article was published, and I received a check for $300.

Mike Plant, a single-handed sailor from Minneapolis, was the sole American entry in the first Vendee Globe, a nonstop, single-handed race around the world. Intrigued that someone from the Midwest would become an ocean sailor, I contacted the editor of his home newspaper, who was also interested and assigned me a number of articles to provide updates during the race. With several additional assignments to cover the race, I approached Delta Air Lines and its partner Air France for travel support. Seeing publicity possibilities, they provided complimentary round-trip air tickets from Seattle to France, where the race would begin and end.

"Race-around-the world" can be questioned because after departing from Les Sables-d'Olonne on France's west coast, the sailors headed due south into the southern latitudes as far as they dared, circumnavigated Antarctica in the frigid waters of the Southern Ocean, and then made a beeline due north to the starting line. Midway through the race, Mike's rigging failed, and he disqualified himself after receiving outside help in New Zealand to replace a damaged five-dollar part. He completed the race anyway and set a new American single-handed circumnavigation record of 135 days.

Sadly, while preparing for the second Vendee race a few years later, Mike was lost at sea. His overturned boat, *Coyote*, was later found floating adrift near the Azores. My articles proved to be source material when Mike's nephew made a documentary movie, *Coyote: The Mike Plant Story*, about his uncle.

When four high school students won honors in an outdoor-writing contest in California, I sent short reports to their hometown newspapers, which they duly published. Even if there's no pay, as in this case, such submissions are a good way to bring one's name to the attention of the editors.

Self-Syndication

I decided to set up my own self-syndication service, which means writing nonexclusive articles for newspapers that serve separate regions. First, using information readily available online, I created for every major North American city a three-tiered database of the largest, second-largest, and third-largest newspapers by circulation.

Because newspapers receive dozens, if not hundreds, of emails daily, I knew I'd get lost in the shuffle if I tried to blanket all of them with a proposed article. Therefore, when I had my first article ready to send, I telephoned each newspaper in the A and B groups to gauge their interest. The how-to books advise against telephoning, but I found it paid off. I quickly eliminated those that said they accept no freelance submissions, syndicated or not.

After culling my database, I was left with good prospects.

How did I manage to telephone 100 or so newspapers in just over one week? As an early riser, I have no trouble starting my Seattle work day at 6 a.m., so I would start making telephone calls to the East Coast newspapers, where it was 9 a.m., asking if there was interest in my article. I'd complete perhaps a dozen calls by 7 a.m. my time, just as the clocks turned 9 a.m. in the Central Time Zone. Now I could start making calls to the Midwest. An hour later I began calling newspapers in the Mountain Time Zone for an hour before the West Coast came to work. And finally I started to telephone newspapers in my own time zone.

Next step was to email the article to newspapers in A group that accepted freelance submissions. A week later I sent the article to the 50 or so newspapers in B group but avoiding those in readership areas where I had received A-group acceptances. After another week, I'd repeat with C group. Once the third group had been sent, there was nothing more to do except wait for responses, and within 10 days or so I received a handful of acceptances with paychecks arriving shortly afterward.

If you want to propose an article for a special edition, say the Hawaii or the cruise ship issue, which have long lead times, editors like to receive a query.

Otherwise, they prefer to have submissions sent "over the transom," meaning that writers send in the complete article with photos at the onset. Don't expect a response anytime soon. It may lie in an editor's in-box for quite a while before anyone decides to use it.

Although this approach worked a number of times with modest success, on one occasion it resulted in a bonanza. When enroute to Hamilton Island Race Week in Australia, my flight passed through Brisbane, the capital of Queensland. Upon descent, I observed a major construction project underway in the outskirts of the city. Inquiring, I learned the city would be hosting World Expo 88, something I hadn't heard about. On my return I stopped for a couple of days to learn about preparations for the upcoming World Fair and interviewed members of the organizing committee. When I explained that I intended to syndicate an article about the World Fair in North America, they gave me 400 slides (no digital photos in 1988) each of three different images—1,200 slides in total—to submit with my story.

The biggest risk to a freelance writer tying to self-syndicate is that one of the wire services (Reuters, AP, and UPI) may beat you by releasing the story to hundreds of subscribing newspapers. To save time, I sent my queries and photos to everyone in the A, B, and C groups of newspapers and hoped for the best.

It took about a week before the first calls came in from editors wanting to authenticate the article; then the rush was on. The wire services had not picked up the story, and every paper wanted mine. Final result: I sold more than 40 articles, each one bringing in between $250 to $400. Expo 88 turned out to be one of the luckiest breaks I ever had.

Takeaway Tips

Stick close to home when writing for newspapers because travel expenses can eat away at the low pay. However, if you're traveling to a destination with expenses covered, seek out local events that may warrant coverage that would be worth your time. Newspapers are always looking for news articles about readers in their circulation area. Finally, if you have ideas for articles of national or international appeal, consider self-syndicating.

10
DIGITAL MEDIA

Think of the internet as the Wild West. There are virtually no rules, no protocols, no standards, no guardianship, very few controls, and no stern-but-fair sheriff to guarantee justice. Anyone can blog or post, meaning it's difficult to establish your credibility among the crowd. You're in the company of amateurs who have not been edited, whose information sources may not be documented, and whose work may be suspect as an advertorial disguised as editorial. Conspiracy theories and so-called fake news abound on the internet. Furthermore, due to immense competition, gaining recognition is difficult. There are approximately two billion websites on the internet and an estimated 505 million blogs with thousands of postings targeting millions of subjects.

I seldom write for the internet because I have had unpleasant experiences with articles being plagiarized and pirated as well as photos being stolen. In addition, digital postings must be kept current, but I don't have the discipline to revise my articles frequently to keep them up to date. Writing for the digital media would also undermine my business model, as explained in Chapter 11.

Despite these disadvantages, you can make money writing for the internet. Here are four of the best ways that I have found.

Personal Blogs

Your blog is a form of personal advertising. You want to use it to sell something or promote a point of view...to attract buyers or sympathetic readers. As a writer, you may want to sell your books, newsletters, pamphlets, research studies, or digital downloads on a subject in your area of expertise. You may also promote your services as a lecturer, keynote speaker, researcher, search-engine optimizer, or writer for hire.

But before sending your message to the world, the first step is to hang out your shingle by creating an attractive, well-named blog website on which to launch your ideas. Then, after you register it, get to work posting your message to the world. And remember to share your posts on social media to broaden your exposure.

To assure readers that you are a real person, your blog website should explain the background that qualifies you as an expert about your subject. You can separate your blog correspondence from personal email by creating a separate email address for the blog domain. To avoid crank calls and harassment, don't list your phone number or street address.

Apart from personal sales you may make or assignments you get, you can make money by advertising products and services of organizations associated with the theme of your blog. If your subject is something like mine, which is winter sports, then ski resorts and outdoor equipment suppliers in these businesses would want to advertise to your blog readers. Ads generate income in three ways: monthly fees, click-through payments, and sales commissions. For a new blogger who has not yet attracted a following, the monthly fee may be low at the onset but can increase as you gain a bigger audience.

Another way to earn income as a blogger is to use Google Adsense, the most popular pay-per-click (PPC) or cost-per-click (CPC) advertising platform. Gaining access to Adsense is free after you establish a free Google account and enter an Adsense code on your blog website. You earn a fee for every reader who clicks through to an advertiser. If a reader subsequently buys one of the advertiser's products, you earn a commission on the sale. To stimulate sales, you may want to write reviews of the advertiser's products.

The key to writing effective blog posts is understanding client expectations as well as those of the target audience. There are many ways to optimize your blog for search engines, but first you need to post well-written, informative posts on a regular basis, say, weekly. It will take a while before your posts show up on search engines, but with the judicious use of target keywords plus blogs posted on a regular schedule, you will soon attract a following to your blog website.

Bloggers for Hire

Many organizations hire bloggers either as employees or independent contractors to promote their services, products, or messages. These establishments include businesses as well as foundations, schools, hospitals, civic groups, trade associations, tourist bureaus, nonprofits, municipalities, and more. These groups want to build their brand and establish rapport with an online audience that will use or support their products.

While large businesses employ in-house bloggers, smaller organizations tend to hire freelancers who are less expensive, offer fast turnaround times, and don't require long-term employment commitments. Another advantage of freelancers is their availability for short-term projects or seasonal work with no obligation to continue.

Freelancers can enter this market by either getting hired as an independent contractor for an organization or by working for a blog management service or agency. As an independent contractor, you need to market yourself directly to organizations where your skills match their needs. If you write outdoor gear reviews, your best chance is to contact companies that cater to hikers, campers, kayakers, or the like. For writers who specialize in travel, you would approach travel agencies and tourism agencies. If personal contact with the client is important, you may be limited to organizations in your geographic region. Negotiations for working on a blog involve agreeing on the length and frequency of the postings. Payment may be based upon a fixed fee for each posting or on a per-word basis with an hourly rate to cover such work as responding to reader inquiries.

If a blog site has not yet been set up, you may be hired to design one and register it. Although this may seem complicated, Word Press offers a convenient platform that can be set up quickly at minimal cost.

How long should a blog post be? There are no absolute rules, but the general minimum is 300 words. Otherwise you'll have too few words to rank in the search engines. Typical is 500–1,500 words depending upon subject matter, and an average is 700–800 words.

Frequency of postings is the other consideration. When starting out, weekly is the usual norm, meaning that your client will have to feed you enough news and updates to give you the material to meet this schedule. If your client is in a seasonal business such as golf in the northern states, you may be asked to post weekly or even daily during the high summer season and then go on hiatus during the winter.

Writers can also approach one of the blog management services. Although you won't make as much money as if you seek out your own markets because these services take a cut of the client's payment, they do all the marketing for you. You can expect to receive assignments that may be short term for a single project and may require an immediate turnaround time. You can expect minimal payment for one short-to-medium-length article, but qualified experts or specialized researchers can earn significantly more. When approaching agencies for a position, emphasize your distinctive skills: technical specialist, press release writer, social media influencer, search-engine optimizer, brand marketer, web page designer, copywriter, gear reviewer, etc.

Apps

Writing an app is similar to writing an extra-long blog without the need for regular updates. Once it's set up and you've promoted it to your potential readership, sit back and wait for followers to be attracted to your site, making occasional revisions as needed from time to time.

To create an app, start by choosing a topic. You should be something of an expert on the subject and able to research to fill in the gaps where your knowledge is lacking. Next you need to make a storyboard, or in app lingo, your *wireframe*, to outline how you want to design and organize the information on every screen. You also need to research your readership to understand what interests them and how best to communicate what you want to say.

Once the wireframe is in hand, you can quickly get tangled in the world of data diagrams, servers, APIs, hosting platforms, and all the related technical jargon. It's important to remember that you're a writer, not a programmer geek. Your job is to create content, not immerse yourself in software details, so find a person or service that will design and build the app and provide hosting. To get your app on the market, you need to create an account with Google Play and Apple Store.

Here's an example of the process. As mentioned, one of my specialties as a freelance journalist is downhill skiing, and for many years I maintained the *Northwest Snowsports Guide* app covering the 50 largest ski areas in five northwestern states (Washington, Oregon, Idaho, Montana, and Wyoming) and two western Canada provinces (British Columbia and Alberta). I contracted with a developer to build the app and incorporate my updates every September when the ski season gets underway. The opening screen summarized my qualifications to write this app and presented filters to the five states and two provinces, as well as to cross-country ski areas, cat ski outfitters, and heliski operators. Each of these links in turn took the reader to write-ups about the ski areas, resorts, and operators. The app gave not only factual information about the ski areas and outfitters, but also insider tips and other information not on the resort website.

You will need to decide if you are going to give your app away and offer ads to generate money, or sell it for download. I charged $5 to access my site and arranged click-through payments, as well as commissions on purchases made through the app.

Influencers

An influencer affects the purchasing decisions of others. Companies in fields ranging from fashion to fishing rods are eager to get their services and products promoted to new audiences, and influencers are the key to getting their messages to the targeted demographics. Many companies retain influencers to coordinate marketing campaigns aimed at sharing key messages with customers. In return for their services, influencers may receive an agreed-upon payment, free products, complimentary travel, vacations, or other benefits.

To establish yourself as an influencer, you must first have a reasonable number of loyal followers who accept you as an authority in your field. In addition to being a credible expert, you must demonstrate you're a leader by identifying trends and projecting what's coming in the future. Once again, it's important to maintain an active presence on Twitter, Facebook, YouTube, Instagram, and other social network platforms.

Uniqueness is an asset. Don't hesitate to be different from—almost to the point of being contrarian to—other writers in your field. Keep launching new ideas and concepts about how your field might be affected by current issues such as climate change, political upheavals, new legislation, and other national or global developments.

11
EVERGREENS

No, this chapter has nothing to do with conifers in the high country. I'm talking about "evergreen" articles: stories and images that are always green and never go out of date. I'll explain how they can make you more money.

When I started out as a freelance writer, I accepted any assignment that came my way. It never occurred to me to choose my job based upon the nature of the article. Whether the assignment was to profile a tourist destination or cover a special event didn't matter. I was glad to get the work regardless of the subject.

Too Much Effort, Too Little Payback

Early on I often covered sailing regattas, following the racing fleet in a chase boat and photographing the action. After the story and images appeared in print, my notes and photos immediately became obsolete and therefore worthless, because regattas in subsequent years featured different sailors and new boat designs. Even when I had multiple assignments and made a reasonable income by covering the event, I could not make further use of the work I had produced.

This same problem came up when I wrote about Mexico and the buildup of the country's west coast marinas. During that time the country underwent a cultural shift that I reflected in my articles. Until the 1980s, Mexico did not have much of a beach culture. Because it's a tropical country, the population prefers the coolness of the mountains rather than the sweltering heat at sea level. All the major cities are inland in the mountains, the sole exception being Veracruz on the Gulf Coast, because it is mainly a shipping port. (When Hernán Cortés landed there in 1519, he had no trouble recruiting into his army the local Indians who, as criminals, had been banished from the cities at higher altitudes.)

Therefore, the country had never built many coastal resorts or recreational marinas. As tourism became a bigger business, Mexico awakened to its coastal development potential. Both the government and private developers began building large marinas on the Pacific Coast to attract not just Mexicans, but also entice U.S. gringos to use as a base for sport-fishing boats, motor cruisers, and sailing yachts. For several years I received assignments every few months to travel up and down the coast to report on and photograph the new construction. My stories ran in several publications, but within weeks of my return home, the information was out of date.

Discover "Evergreens"

I soon realized that my images and articles could be long-term investments if I chose assignments more intelligently. That's when I began to write evergreen articles: stories with images that never go out of date. Tropical beaches don't change over time. Neither do natural landscapes, happy faces, or beautiful sunsets. Consequently, since then I have seldom written about sailing regattas or time-specific events. Instead, I sell updated evergreen articles with photos from assignments that may have been fulfilled more than a decade earlier.

My first article about sailing in Tahiti has been published perhaps a dozen times since I made the initial cruise some 20 years ago. Each time before I pitch it to a new publication, I send emails to my sources to freshen quotes, update facts, and renew my perspective. Otherwise this original article has changed little since I first wrote it.

I also have evergreen features about bareboat sailing in the British Virgin Islands, where I have cruised perhaps 20 times over the years. Because the main parts of the articles are already written, when I'm hosted on a three-day assignment it takes only half a day to freshen them, which leaves more time to sail with friends and family.

Annual Events

Sometimes I accept assignments to cover an event if it's one I enjoy, and it's an annual occurrence. For example, I used to participate in the weeklong Baja-Ha-Ha Cruisers Rally that in its original form took place at Partida Island 20 miles off the coast of La Paz, Mexico. Although the boats and crews were always in flux, I could salvage enough information and photos from previous visits to incorporate into the current articles. In my early years I scurried around interviewing people, gathering information, and taking photos, but in later years I could relax and spend more time participating in the festivities.

I also reused earlier information and photos from my many trips to Hamilton Island Race Week in Australia's Whitsunday Islands. My photos of the famous silica-sand Whitehaven Beach taken the first year were current 20 years later, and it took minimal effort to update aspects of the event that had changed little over the years. I loved this assignment because the courtesy cruising yacht my host provided was not only a place to sleep, but also offered the opportunity to explore what are arguably the most wonderful sailing waters anywhere on the planet. Whether visiting luxurious Hayman Island, backpackers' Hook Island, or an isolated cove at Lindeman Island, I have never tired of this mini-paradise at the gateway to the Great Barrier Reef.

Sometimes I make a trip to a destination that I probably won't revisit, so I approach the subject in a different way to make it an evergreen article. Such was my journey to two of Italy's most famous ski resorts, Cortina d'Ampezzo and Val Gardena in the Dolomites. In addition to interviewing key people at the ski area, I collected their contact information and told them they would likely hear from me in the years ahead as I updated my information. I photographed the five towers of the famous Cinque Torri formations from different angles and stayed on the mountain late into the afternoon to catch images of the setting sun illuminating the rose-tinted mountains, knowing I could sell these images for years to come. Unfortunately, sections of the towers have been collapsing in recent years, so my photos may soon become dated.

The combined ski area, said to be the largest in the world, is dotted with 42 restaurants, so I took extended lunch breaks to photograph the local cuisine coming out of the kitchens as well as shots of happy skiers seated on the outdoor decks enjoying their noontime meal and wine. Many restaurants had been around for more than 100 years, so I felt confident they'd continue for another century, and I could use my images well into the future. Likewise, traditional recipes handed down by generations of grandmas don't change. I did close-up photos of Ampezzan specialties such as casunziei, half-moon-shaped pasta stuffed with beets. Years later I'm refreshing the quotes and still recycling these articles.

Scuba diving articles are almost always evergreens because sea creatures, underwater foliage, and coral look the same as they did hundreds of years ago. Scuba gear has changed little in recent years, so images of divers taken a decade ago look as current as they do today. Sadly though, I have to stay updated about coral bleaching, because reef deterioration is rapidly increasing around the globe due to warming of the oceans. Another threat is the invasion of lionfish at favorite dive sites. These voracious eaters of other fish have no natural predators in the Atlantic or Caribbean.

Nowhere has the concept of evergreens served me better than for articles about downhill skiing in the western U.S. and Canada where I regularly ski at more than 75 ski resorts. Beginning in the mid-1990s I began publishing, in conjunction with a small outdoor magazine, the 40-page *Western Snowsports Guide* that gives annual updates on every major ski resort in the western U.S. states and Canadian provinces. By the end of the second season I had researched all the background of every resort. In subsequent years I reused the same material, adding only a sentence or two to report any updates such as a new ski lift, an additional lodge, or new ski trails. This left more time to appreciate the slopes.

Sell Only One-Time Print Rights

When offering an article to a publication, I have to be clear I am selling only one-time print rights, not reprint rights and certainly not the right to post on the publication's website. The heart of my business model is reselling articles as evergreens, but once they're posted online, I can't reuse them. This is why written contracts can be difficult. If I receive a contract to sign, I know it won't do any good to argue with the publication's lawyers whose job is to assure their organization gets everything it asks for. What I do, and there has seldom been a problem, is to strike out and initial any reference to reprint and internet rights and send it back to the editor. Once received, the editor is satisfied I have signed and doesn't look further. If later the publication posts my article online, I protest and point out what I had stricken in the contract. On a few occasions, discussions have become testy, at which point we agree to something like posting an article for only three months and then taking it down.

Update Facts

Sometimes an evergreen article loses its immortality. For years I recycled a piece about an isolated beach on the southwestern coast of Maui. I had camped at Makena Beach with my family years earlier, and each time before reselling my article, I would get updates by contacting a friend who lives in the area. For many years the site remained pristine. One day, just as I was about to send the updated article to an outdoors magazine, he informed me that bulldozers were in the area, and a luxury hotel was under construction. That evergreen suddenly turned brown and died.

Evergreen Guidelines

The guidelines for writing evergreen articles are simple: avoid dated subjects and events, avoid stories that are still unfolding, and avoid photos of dated styles and work in progress. Today I have 25 to 30 evergreen articles that I continually sell to different publications, enough to keep me busy even if I never write another new article.

12
PUTTING IT ALL TOGETHER

Although my approach to freelance writing is contrary to many recommendations in the how-to books, it's been successful for me. Here are some high points:

Travel Expenses

Arranging free travel gets me to interesting corners of the globe, where I seek out stories that few know about. First, I look for press trips to a destination that has potential for interesting story ideas. If there aren't any press trips, I contact airlines, resort hotels, and visitors bureaus and ask them to sponsor me. If this doesn't work, I leverage accumulated frequent-flyer miles and hotel award points for my globetrotting.

Multiple Queries

When pitching a story, rather than sending queries one at a time, I send multiple queries. If two or more publications accept, I write two articles with different slants so each publication has rights to a unique article.

Self-Syndication

In markets with multiple daily papers, I have a newspaper data base broken into three tiers by circulation. I send stories first to the larger publications and subsequently to the smaller ones.

Evergreens

I maintain an inventory of 25 to 30 evergreen articles that I send out continuously, freshening and updating them each time.

Unusual Article Ideas

I veer from the beaten media path to find subjects on those unpaved trails that few people have discovered. I'm often on an adventure of my own, having fun investigating new subjects and getting exclusive stories.

Photos

I carry a camera on every assignment, even when a professional photographer is assigned to me, and my shots often get published rather than the pro's. Images can increase revenue by 50 to 100 percent.

Multiple Assignments

I accept only assignments with a potential for a minimum of three articles.

Competition Avoidance

I avoid highly publicized events and find stories that few people know about.

Writers Organizations

I belong to several professional writers' organizations and attend their conferences, where I contact editors, meet newsmakers, and benefit from craft-improvement presentations.

Income Objective

Because I keep my evergreen articles in constant circulation, I comfortably earn an income equal to that of a midlevel business executive. But if I put a value on all the airline tickets, resort accommodations and meals, tourist bureau perks, outfitter services, and equipment such as chartered yachts, scuba gear, rental cars, and outfitter packages provided at no cost, my salary exceeds that of many high-level corporate managers.

Enjoyable Lifestyle

I work the hours and days I prefer and take time off whenever I want. No boss, no policies, no boring office setting.

Work from Home

No commute. No dress codes. No endless meetings. No hovering bosses. Home-office tax deductions are an important cost savings.

Equip Your Office

Computer, printer, recorder, writing software, camera, office supplies.

Quick Writing Fixes

- Avoid passive voice, being verbs, adjectives, and adverbs.

- Power is in the verbs.

- Replace "which" with "that" if possible, and drop "that" whenever you can.

- Vary rhythm in sentences.

- Strong ledes at the beginning kick the reader into the story, and reinforcing kickers at the end kick the story into the reader.

- Use quotes for feelings and emotions, not facts.

- Avoid simple subject-verb-object sentences.

Interns

Journalism students seeking internships can be invaluable in helping you research markets for both evergreens and new assignments. In return, they get scholastic credit and learn how to be successful freelance writers.

In Closing

I've been successful in approaching my work in a way that is both financially and personally rewarding. The reason for my success? My approach is often the opposite of what other freelance writers do. I feel a little like the guy who's driving home after work and gets a call on his cell phone from his wife. "Honey, I just heard on the news that some guy is driving the wrong way on the freeway, so be careful." He replies, "Yeah, I know. And it's not just one guy. There are hundreds of them."

THE END

ABOUT THE AUTHOR

With degrees from Princeton University and University of New Mexico, Peter Schroeder began his career in nuclear weapons design, development, and testing. However, he soon became disillusioned with this work and decided to pursue his dream of becoming a freelance outdoor adventure travel writer.

After several years following the advice of the "how-to" books, he realized they were all wrong and practically guaranteed one could never earn a decent living.

Instead, he applied skills learned while earning an MBA Degree at Stanford's Graduate School of Business. Soon, he was earning a significant income. Paradoxically, his approach was directly opposite to the advice of the so-called "how-to" books. Utilizing the techniques he developed, Schroeder succeeded as a freelancer throughout his 30-year career. He has written several hundred articles about downhill skiing, scuba diving, cruising under sail, and adventure travel for newspapers and magazines in North America and abroad. In addition, he is the author of several books.

Having proved that his unorthodox ideas worked, he went on the lecture circuit, speaking to writers' organizations across the country. His presentations received accolades, and colleagues suggested he put his ideas into a book...

... Which is what you now hold in your hands.